Blackburn Henry

Artists and Arabs

Sketching in Sunshine

Blackburn Henry

Artists and Arabs
Sketching in Sunshine

ISBN/EAN: 9783744760195

Printed in Europe, USA, Canada, Australia, Japan

Cover: Foto ©Thomas Meinert / pixelio.de

More available books at **www.hansebooks.com**

Artists and Arabs;

OR,

SKETCHING IN SUNSHINE.

BY

HENRY BLACKBURN,

AUTHOR OF "NORMANDY PICTURESQUE," "ART IN THE MOUNTAINS,"
"TRAVELLING IN SPAIN," "THE PYRENEES," ETC.

With Numerous Illustrations.

BOSTON:
ESTES AND LAURIAT,
301 WASHINGTON STREET.
1878.

CONTENTS.

LIST OF ILLUSTRATIONS.

ARGUMENT.

The advantage of winter studios in the South, and the value of sketching in the open air, especially in Algeria.

"The best thing the author of a book can do, is to tell the reader, on a piece of paper an inch square, what he means by it." — *Athenæum*.

Artists and Arabs

or

Sketching in Sunshine

ARTISTS AND ARABS.

CHAPTER I.

ON THE WING.

BY the middle of the month of July the Art season in London was on the wane, and by the end of August the great body of English artists had dispersed, some, the soundest workers perhaps, to the neighborhood of Welsh mountains and English homesteads, to "the silence of thatched cottages and the voices of blossoming fields."

From the Tweed to the Shetland Isles they were thick upon the hills; in every nook and corner of England, amongst the cornfields and upon the lakes; in the valleys and torrent beds of Wales, the cry was still "they come."

On the continent of Europe both artists and amateurs were everywhere. Smith, toiling across the Campagna with the thermometer at 90, his reward a quiet pipe at the "café Grecco" when the sun goes down, is but a counterpart of a hundred other Smiths scattered abroad. In the galleries of Florence and Rome no more easels could be admitted, and in Switzerland and Savoy the little white tents and sun-umbrellas glistened on the mountain-side. Brown might be seen rattling down an arrête from the Flegère, with his *matériel* swung across his back like a carpenter's basket, after a hard day's work sketching the Aiguilles that tower above the valley of Chamounix; and Jones, with his little wife beside him, sitting under the deep shade of the beech-trees in the valley of Sixt.

We were a sketching party, consisting of two, three, or four, according to convenience or accident, wandering about and pitching our tent in various places away from the track of tourists ; we had been spending most of the summer days in the beautiful Val d'Aosta (that school for realistic work that a great teacher once selected for his pupil, giving him three months to study its chestnut groves, "to brace his mind to a comprehension of facts"); we had prolonged the summer far into autumn on the north shore of the Lago Maggiore, where from the heights above the old towns of Intra and Pallanza we had watched its banks turn from green to golden and from gold to russet brown. The mountains were no longer *en toilette*, as the French express it, and the vineyards were stripped of their purple bloom ; the wind had come down from the Simplon in sudden and determined gusts, and Monte Rosa no longer stood alone in her robe of white ; the last visitor had left the Hôtel de l'Univers at Pallanza, and our host was glad to entertain us at the rate of

four francs a day "tout compris," — when the
question came to us, as it does to so many other
wanderers in Europe towards the end of October,
where to go for winter quarters, where to steal
yet a further term of summer days.

Should we go again to Spain to study Velasquez
and Murillo, should we go as usual to Rome, or
should we strike out a new path altogether and
go to Trebizond, Cairo, Tunis, or Algeria? There
was no agreeing on the matter, diversity of opinion
was great and discussion ran high (the majority,
we must own, having leanings towards Rome and
chic, and also "because there would be more
fun"); so, like true Bohemians, we tossed for
places and the lot fell upon Algeria.

The next morning we are on the way. Trusting ourselves to one of those frail-looking little
boats with white awnings, that form a feature in
every picture of Italian lake-scenery, and which,
in their peculiar motion and method of propulsion

(the rower standing at the stern and facing his work), bear just sufficient resemblance to the Venetian gondola to make us chafe a little at the slow progress we make through the water, we sit and watch the receding towers of Pallanza, as it seems, for the livelong day. There is nothing to relieve the monotony of motion, and scarcely a sound to break the stillness, until we approach the southern shore, and it becomes a question of anxiety as to whether we shall really reach Arona before sundown. But the old boatman is not to be moved by any expostulation or entreaty, nor is he at all affected by the information that we run great risk of losing the last train from Arona; and so we are spooned across the great deep lake at the rate of two or three miles an hour, and glide into the harbor with six inches of water on the flat bottom of the boat amongst our portmanteaus.

From Arona to Genoa by railway, and from Genoa to Nice by the Cornice road, — that most

beautiful of all drives, where every variety of
grandeur and loveliness of view, both by sea and
land, seems combined, and from the heights of
which, if we look seaward and scan the southern
horizon, we can sometimes trace an irregular dark
line, which is Corsica, — past Mentone and Nice,
where the " winter swallows " are arriving fast,
making a wonderful flutter in their nests, all eagerness to obtain the most comfortable quarters, and
all anxiety to have none but " desirable " swallows
for neighbors. This last is a serious matter, this
settling down for the winter at Nice, for it is here
that the swallows choose their mates, pairing off
quietly in the springtime, — who knows whither?

A few hours' journey by railway and we are
at Marseilles, where (especially at the " Grand
Hotel ") it is an understood and settled thing that
every Englishman is on his way to Italy or India.
It requires considerable perseverance to impress
upon the attendants that the steamer which sails

at noon for Algiers is the one on which our baggage is to be placed, and it is almost impossible to persuade the driver of a fiacre that we do *not* want to go by the boat just starting for Civita Vecchia or Leghorn.

On stepping on board the *Akhbar* it almost seems as if there were some mistake, for we appear to be the only passengers on the after-deck, and are looked upon with some curiosity by the swarthy, half-naked crew, who talk together in an unknown tongue. We have several hours to wait and to look about us, for the mail is not brought on board until three in the afternoon, and it is at least half past before the officials have kissed each other on both cheeks, and we are really moving off, — threading our way with difficulty through the mass of shipping which hems us in on all sides.

The foredeck of the *Akhbar* is one mass of confusion and crowding, but the eye soon detects the first blush of Oriental color and costume, and it is easy to distinguish a white bournous moving in a stately manner through the crowd. There are plenty of Zouaves in undress uniforms, chiefly young men, with a superfluity of medals, and the peculiar swagger which seems inseparable from this costume ; others old and bronzed, who have been to Europe on leave, and are returning to join their regiments. Some parting scenes we witness between families of the peasant order, of whom there appear to be a number on board. These, one and all, take leave of each other with a significant " au revoir," which is the key-note to the whole business, and tells us (who have no wish or intention to trouble the reader with the history or prospects of the colony) the secret of its ill-success, viz. : that these colonists *intend to come back*, and that they are much too near home in Algeria.

Looking down upon the foredeck, as we leave the harbor of Marseilles, there seems scarcely an available inch of space that is not encumbered with bales and goods of all. kinds ; with heaps of rope and chain, military stores, piles of arms, cavalry-horses, sheep, pigs, and a prodigious number of live fowls. On the after-deck there are but six passengers besides ourselves : there is a Moorish Jew talking fluently with a French commercial traveller, a sad and silent officer of Chasseurs with his young wife, and two lieutenants who chatter away with the captain ; the latter, in consideration of his rank as an officer in the Imperial Marine, leaving the mate to take charge of the vessel during the entire voyage. This gentleman seems to the uninitiated to be a curious encumbrance, and to pass his time in conversation, in sleep, and in the consumption of bad cigars. He is "a disappointed man" of course, as all naval officers are, of whatever nation, age, or degree.

The voyage averages forty-eight hours, but is often accomplished in less time on the southward journey. It is an uncomfortable period even in fine weather, just too long for a pleasure-trip, and just too short to settle down and make up one's mind to it, as in crossing the Atlantic. Our boat is an old Scotch "screw," which has been lent to the Company of the *Messageries Impériales* for winter duty, — the shaft hammering and vibrating through the saloon and after-cabins incessantly for the first twenty-four hours, whilst she labors against a cross-sea in the Gulf of Lyons. About noon on the next day it becomes calm, and the *Akhbar* steams quietly between the Balearic Islands, close enough for us to distinguish one or two churches and white houses, and a square erection that a fellow-traveller informs us is the work of the "Majorca Land, Compagnie Anglaise."

In the following little sketch we have indicated the appearance in outline of the two islands of Majorca and Minorca as we approach them going southward, passing at about equal distances between the islands.

The sea is calm and the sky is bright as we leave the islands behind us, and the *Akhbar* seems to plough more easily through the deep blue water, leaving a wake of at least a mile, and another wake in the sky of sea-gulls, who follow us for the rest of the voyage in a graceful undulating line, sleeping on the rigging at night unmolested by the crew, who believe in the good omen.

On the second morning on coming on deck we find ourselves in the tropics; the sky is a deep azure, the heat is intense, and the brightness of everything is wonderful. The sun's rays pour down on the vessel, and their effect on the occupants of the foredeck is curious to witness. The odd heaps of clothing that had lain almost unnoticed during the voyage suddenly come to life,

and here and there a dark visage peeps from under a tarpaulin, from the inside of a coil of rope, or from a box of chain. Soon the whole vessel, both the fore and after deck, is teeming with life, and we find at least double the number of human beings on board that we had had any idea of at starting.

But the interest of every one is now centred on a low dark line of coast, with a background of mountains, which every minute becomes more defined ; and we watch it until we can discern one or two of the highest peaks, tipped with snow. Soon we can make out a bright green, or rather, as it seems in the sunlight, a golden shore, set with a single gem that sparkles in the water. Again it changes into the aspect of a white pyramid or triangle of chalk resting on the sea ; next, into an irregular mass of houses with flat roofs, and mosques with ornamented towers and cupolas, surrounded and surmounted by grim fortifications,

which are not Moorish; and in a little while we
can distinguish the French houses and hotels, a
Place, a modern harbor and lighthouse, docks, and
French shipping, and one piratical-looking craft
that passes close under our bows, manned by dark
sailors with bright red sashes and large ear-rings,
dressed like the fishermen in the opera of Masa-
niello. And whilst we are watching and taking
it all in, we have glided to our moorings, close
under the walls of the great Mosque (part of which
we have sketched from this very point of view);
and are surrounded by a swarm of half-naked,
half-wild, and frantic figures, who rush into the
water vociferating and imploring us, in languages
difficult to understand, to be permitted to carry
the Franks' baggage to the shore.

Taking the first that comes, we are soon at the
landing-steps and beset by a crowd of beggars,
touters, idlers, and nondescripts of nearly every
nation and creed under heaven.

2

LA FILLE DU CORSAIRE.

CHAPTER II.

ALGIERS.

"Ah oui, c'est qu'elle est belle avec ces châteaux forts,
  Couchés dans les près verts, comme les géants morts !
  C'est qu'elle est noble, ALGER la fille du corsaire !
  Un réseau de murs blancs la protége et l'enserre."

THE first view of the town of Algiers, with its clusters of white houses set in bright green hills, — or, as the French express it, "like a diamond set in emeralds," the range of the lesser Atlas forming a background of purple waves rising one above the other until they are lost in cloud, — was perhaps the most beautiful sight we had witnessed, and it is as well to record it at once, lest the experience of the next few hours might banish it from memory.

It was a good beginning to have a stately bare-footed Arab to shoulder our baggage from the port, and wonderful to see the load he carried unassisted. As he winds his way through the narrow and steep slippery streets (whilst we who are shod by Hoby and otherwise encumbered by broadcloth have enough to do to keep pace with him, and indeed to keep our footing), it is good to see how nobly our Arab bears his load, how beautifully balanced is his lithe figure, and with what grace and ease he stalks along. As he bows slightly, when taking our three francs (his "tariff" as he calls it), there is a dignity in his manner, and a composure about him that is almost embarrassing. How he came, in the course of circumstances, to be carrying our luggage instead of wandering with his tribe, perhaps civilization — French civilization — can answer.

The first hurried glance (as we followed our cicerone up the landing-steps to a large French

hotel facing the sea) at the dazzlingly white flat-
roofed houses without windows, at the mosques
with their gayly painted towers, at the palm-trees
and orange-trees, and at the crowd of miscellaneous
costumes, in which bright colors preponderated,
gave the impression of a thorough Mohammedan
city; and now as we walk down to the *Place* and
look about us at leisure, we find to our astonish-
ment and delight that the Oriental element is still
most prominent.

The most striking and bewildering thing is undoubtedly the medley that meets the eye everywhere : the conflict of races, the contrast of colors,
the extraordinary brightness of everything, the
glare, the strange sounds and scenes that cannot
be easily taken in at a first visit; the variety of
languages heard at the same time, and above all
the striking beauty of some faces, and the luxurious richness of costume.

First in splendor come the Moors (traders look-

ing like princes), promenading or lounging about
under the trees, looking as important and as richly
attired as ever was Caliph Haroun Alraschid.
They are generally fair and slight of figure, with
false, effeminate faces, closely shaven heads covered
with fez and turban, loose baggy white trousers, and
jacket and vest of blue or crimson cloth embroidered with gold ; round their waists are rich silken
sashes, and their fingers are covered with a profusion of rings. Their legs are bare to the knee,
and their feet are enclosed in Turkish slippers.

This is the prominent town type of Moor or
Jew, the latter to be distinguished by wearing
dark trousers, clean white stockings, French shoes,
and a round cloth cap of European pattern. There
are various grades, both of the Moors and Jews,
some of course shabby and dirty enough ; but the
most dignified and picturesque figures are the tall
dark Arabs and the Kabyles, remarkable for their
independent, noble bearing, their flowing white

bournouses, and their turbans of camel's hair.
Here we see them walking side by side with their
conquerors in full military uniform and with their
conquerors' wives in the uniform of *Le Follet*,
whilst white-robed female figures flit about closely
veiled, and Marabouts (the Mohammedan priests)
also promenade in their flowing robes. Arab
women and children lounge about selling fruit or
begging furtively, and others hurry to and fro
carrying burdens ; and everywhere and ever present in this motley throng, the black frock-coat
and chimney-pot of civilization assert themselves,
to remind us of what we might otherwise soon be
forgetting, — that we are but four days' journey
from England.

There is noise enough altogether on the *Place*
to bewilder any stranger ; for besides the talking
and singing, and the cries of vendors of fruit and
wares, there is considerable traffic. Close to us
as we sit under the trees (so close as almost to

upset the little tables in front of the cafés), and without any warning, a huge diligence comes lunging on to the *Place*, groaning under a pile of merchandise, with a bevy of Arabs on the roof, and a party of Moorish women in the "rotonde"; presently there passes a company of Zouaves at quick step, looking hot and dusty enough, marching to their terrible tattoo; and next, by way of contrast again, come two Arab women with their children, mounted on camels, the beasts looking overworked and sulky, as they edge their way through the crowd with the greatest nonchalance, and with an impatient croaking sound go shambling past.

The "Place Royale" faces the north, and is enclosed on three sides with modern French houses with arcades and shops, the contents of which are principally French. Next door to a bonnet-shop there is certainly the name of Mustapha over the door, and in the window are pipes, coral, and filagree work exposed for sale; but most of the goods come from France. Next door again is a French café, where Arabs, who can afford it, delight in being waited upon by their conquerors in white aprons and neckties. The background of all this is superb: a calm sunlit sea, white sails glittering and flashing, and far to the eastward a noble bay, with the Kabyle mountains stretching out their arms towards the north.

At four o'clock the band plays on the *Place*, and as we sit and watch the groups of Arabs and Moors listening attentively to the overture to " William Tell," or admiringly examining the gay uniforms and medals of the Chasseurs d'Afrique; as we see the children of both nations at high romps together; as the sweet sea-breeze that fans us so gently bears into the newly constructed harbor together a corvette of the French Marine and a suspicious-looking raking craft with latteen sails; as Marochetti's equestrian statue of the Duke of Orleans and a mosque stand side by side before us, — we have Algiers presented to us in the easiest way imaginable, and, without going through the ordeal of studying its history or statistics, obtain some idea of the general aspect of the place and the people, and of the relative position of conquerors and conquered.

As our business is principally with the Moorish, or picturesque side of things, let us first look at the great Mosque which we glanced at as we entered the harbor. Built close to the water's edge, so close that the Mediterranean waves are sapping its foundations, with plain white shining walls, nearly destitute of exterior ornament, it is perhaps the most perfect example of strength and beauty, and of fitness and grace of line, that we shall see in any building of this type.* It is

* This beautiful architectural feature of the town has not escaped the civilizing hand of the Frank ; the last time we visited Algiers we found the oval window in the tower gone, and in its place an illuminated French clock!

thoroughly Moorish in style, although built by a
Christian, if we may believe the story, of which
there are several versions : how the Moors in old
days took captive a Christian architect, and promised him his liberty on condition of his building them a mosque ; how he, true to his own
creed, dexterously introduced into the ground plan
the form of a cross ; and how the Moors, true also
to their promise, gave him his liberty indeed, but
at the cannon's mouth through a window, seaward.

The general outline of these mosques is familiar
to most readers, the square white walls pierced at
intervals with narrow little windows, the flat cu-
pola, or dome, and the square tower often standing
apart from the rest of the structure like an Italian campanile, as in the illustration given on page
124. Some of these towers are richly decorated
with arabesque ornamentation, and glitter in the
sun with color and gilding ; but exterior decoration is quite the exception, the majority of the

mosques being as plain and simple in design as in our illustration.

Here, if we take off our shoes, we may enter and hear the Koran read, and we may kneel down to pray with Arabs and Moors; religious tolerance is equally exercised by both creeds. Altogether the Mohammedan places of worship seem by far the most prominent, and although there is a Roman Catholic church and buildings held by other denominations of Christians, there is none of that predominant proselytizing aspect which we might have expected after thirty years' occupation by the French. At Tetuan, for instance, where the proportion of Christians to Mohammedans is certainly smaller, the "Catholic church" rears its head much more conspicuously. In Algiers the priestly element is undoubtedly active, and *Sœurs de Charité* are to be seen everywhere, but the buildings that first strike the eye are mosques rather than churches; the sounds that become more familiar to the ear than peals of bells are the Muezzins' morning and evening salutation from the tower of a mosque, calling upon all true believers to

> "Come to prayers, come to prayers,
> It is better to pray than to sleep."

The principal streets in Algiers lead east and west from the *Place* to the principal gates, the Bab-Azoun and the Bab-el-Oued. They are for the most part French, with arcades like the Rue de Rivoli in Paris; many of the houses are lofty, and built in the style best known in Europe as the "Haussman." Nearly all the upper town is Moorish, and is approached by narrow streets or lanes, steep, slippery, and tortuous, which we shall examine by and by.*

The names of some of the streets are curious,

---

* It may be interesting to artists to learn that in this present year, 1873, many of the quaintest old Moorish streets and buildings are intact ; neither disturbed by earthquakes nor "improved" out of sight.

and suggestive of change. Thus we see the "Rue Royale," the "Rue Impériale"; there is a "Place Nationale," and one street is still boldly proclaimed to be the "Rue de la Révolution"!

In passing through the French quarter, through the new wide streets, squares, and inevitable boulevards, the number of shops for fancy goods and Parisian wares, especially those of hair-dressers and modistes, seems rather extraordinary, remembering that the entire European population of Algeria, agricultural as well as urban, is not more than 150,000. In a few shops there are tickets displayed in different languages, but linguists are rare, and where there are announcements of
INGLIS SPOKEN. the labels have generally a perplexing, composite character, like the inscription on a statue at the Paris Exhibition of 1867, which ran thus, "Miss Ofelia dans Amlet."

Let us now glance at the general mode of living in Algiers, speaking first of the traveller who

goes to the hotels. The ordinary visitor of a
month or two will drop down pleasantly enough
into the system of hotel life in Algiers; and even
if staying for the winter he will probably find it
more convenient and amusing to take his meals
in French fashion at the hotels, ringing the
changes between three or four of the best, and
one or two well-known cafés. There is generally no table-d'hôte, but strangers can walk in
and have breakfast or dine very comfortably at
little tables "*à part*," at fixed hours, at a moder-
ate price. The rooms are pleasant, cool, and airy,
with large windows open to the sea. Everything
is neatly and quietly served, the menu is varied
enough, with good French dishes and game in
abundance; the hosts being especially liberal in
providing those delicious little birds that might
be larks or quails, which in Algiers we see so
often at table and so seldom on the wing.

Half the people that are dining at the "Hôtel

d'Orient" to-day are residents or habitués; they
come in and take their accustomed places as
coseyly, and are almost as particular and fastidious
as if they were at their club.   There is the colonel
of a cavalry regiment dining alone, and within
joking distance five young officers, whose various
grades of rank are almost as evident from their
manner as from the number of stripes on their
bright red *kepis* ranged on the wall of the salon.
A French doctor and his wife dine vis-à-vis at
one table, a lady *solitaire* at another, and some
gentlemen, whose minds are tuned to commerce,
chatter in a corner by themselves; whilst a group
of newly arrived English people in the middle of
the room are busily engaged in putting down the
various questions with which they intend to bore
the vice-consul on the morrow, as if he were some
good-natured house-agent, valet-de-place, and in-
terpreter in one, placed here by Providence for
their especial behoof.   But it is all very orderly,

sociable, and comfortable, and by no means an unpleasant method of living for a time.

There is the *cercle*, the club, at which we may dine sometimes; there are those pretty little villas amongst the orange-trees at Mustapha Supérieure, where we may spend the most delightful evenings of all; and there are also the Governor's weekly balls, soirées at the consulate, and other pleasant devices for turning night into day, in Algiers as everywhere else, which we shall be wise if we join in but sparingly; and there are public amusements, concerts, balls, and the theatre, —the latter with a company of operatic singers with weak lungs, but voices as sweet as any heard in Italy; and there are the moonlight walks by the sea, to many the greatest delight of all.

The ordinary daily occupations are decidedly social and domestic; and it may be truly said that for a stranger, until he becomes accustomed to the place, there is very little going on. You must not bathe, for instance, on this beautiful shelving shore. "Nobody bathes, it gives fever," was the invariable answer to inquiries on this subject; and, though it is not absolutely forbidden by the faculty, there are so many restrictions imposed upon bathers that few attempt it; moreover, an Englishman is not likely to have brought an acrobatic suit with him, nor will he easily find a "costume de bain" in Algiers.

There is very little to do besides wander about the town, or make excursions in the environs or into the interior, in which latter case it is as well to take a fowling-piece, as there is plenty of game to be met with; and altogether we may answer a question often asked about Algiers as to its attractions for visitors, that it has not many (so called) for the mere holiday lounger. But for those who have resources of their own, who have work to do which they wish to do quietly, and who breathe more freely under a bright blue sky, Algiers seems to us to be *the* place to come to.

The "bird of passage," who has unfortunately missed an earthquake, often reports that Algiers is a little dull; but even he should not find it so, for, beyond the "distractions" we have hinted at, there is plenty to amuse him if he care little for what is picturesque. There are (or were when we were there) a troop of performing Arabs of the tribe of "Beni Zouzoug," who performed nightly the most hideous atrocities in the name of religious rites : wounding their wretched limbs with knives, eating glass, holding burning coals in their mouths, standing on hot iron until the feet frizzled and gave forth sickening odors, and doing other things in an ecstasy of religious frenzy which we could not print, and which would scarcely be believed in if we did.*

There are various Moorish ceremonies to be

* Since writing the above, we observe that these Arabs (or a band of mountebanks in their name) have been permitted to perform their horrible orgies in Paris and London, and that young ladies go in evening dress to the "stalls" to witness them.

witnessed.   There are the sacrifices at the time
of the Ramadhan, when the negro priestesses go
down to the water side and offer up beasts and
birds ; the victims, after prolonged agonies which
crowds assemble to witness, being finally handed
over to a French *chef de cuisine.*   There, are the
mosques, to be entered barefoot, and the native
courts of law to be seen.   Then, if possible, a
Moor should be visited at home, and a glimpse
obtained of his domestic economy, including a
dinner without knives or forks.

An entertainment consisting entirely of Moorish dances and music is easily got up, and is one
of the characteristic sights of Algiers.   The young
trained dancing-girls, urged on to frenzy by the
beating of the tom-tom, and falling exhausted at
last into the arms of their masters, dancing with
that monotonous motion peculiar to the East, the
body swaying to and fro without moving the feet,
the uncouth, wild airs they sing, their shrieks

dying away into a sigh or moan, will not soon be forgotten, and many other scenes of a like nature, on which we must not dwell, — for are they not written in twenty books on Algeria already?

But there are two sights which are seldom mentioned by other writers, which we must just allude to in passing. The Arab races, which take place in the autumn on the French race-course near the town, are very curious, and well worth seeing. Their peculiarity consists in about thirty Arabs starting off pell-mell, knocking each other over in their first great rush, their bournouses mingling together and flying in the wind, but arriving at the goal generally singly, and at a slow trot, in anything but racing fashion. Another event is the annual gathering of the tribes, when representatives from the various provinces camp on the hills of the Sahel, and the European can wander from one tent to another and spend his day enjoying Arab hospitality, in sipping coffee and smoking everywhere the pipe of peace.

These things we only hint at as resources for visitors, if they are fortunate enough to be in Algiers at the right time; but there are one or two other things that they are not likely to miss, whether they wish to do so or not.

They will probably meet one day, in the "Street of the Eastern Gate," the Sirocco wind, and they will have to take shelter from a sudden fearful darkness and heat, a blinding, choking dust, drying up as it were the very breath of life, penetrating every cavity, and into rooms closed as far as possible from the outer air. Man and beast lie down before it, and there is a sudden silence in the streets, as if they had been overwhelmed by the sea. For two or three hours this mysterious blight pours over the city, and its inhabitants hide their heads.

Another rather startling sensation for the first time is the "morning gun." In the consulate, which is in an old Moorish house in the upper town,

the newly arrived visitor may have been shown
imbedded in the wall a large round shot, which
he is informed was a messenger from one of Lord
Exmouth's three-deckers in the days before the
French occupation; and not many yards from it,
in another street, he may have had pointed out
to him certain fissures or chasms in the walls of
the houses, as the havoc made by earthquakes;
he may also have experienced in his travels the
sudden and severe effect of a tropical thunder-
storm. Let him retire to rest with a dreamy
recollection of such events in his mind, and let
him have his windows open towards the port just
before sunrise, — when the earthquake and the
thunder and the bombardment will present themselves so suddenly and fearfully to his sleepy
senses, that he will bear malice against the military governor forevermore.

But it has roused him to see another of the
sights of Algiers. Let him go out at once in the

dim morning light to the almost deserted *Place*,
where a few tall figures wrapped in military cloaks
are to be seen sidling out of a door in the corner
of a square under the arcades, — coming from the
club where the gas is not quite extinguished, and
where the little green baize tables are not yet
put away for the night ; * and then let him hurry
on to the *Bab-el-Oued* and mount the fortifications, and he will see a number of poor Arabs
shivering in their white bournouses, perched on
the highest points of the rocks like eagles, watching with eager eyes and strained aspect for the
rising of the sun, for "the coming of the second
Mahomet."   Let him look in the same direction,
eastward, over the town and over the bay to the

* How often have we seen in the Tuileries gardens the
bronzed heroes of Algerian wars, and perhaps have pitied them
for their worn appearance ; but we shall begin to think that
something more than the African sun and long marches have
given them a prematurely aged appearance, and that absinthe
and late hours in a temperature of 90° Fahrenheit may have
something to do with it.

mountains far beyond. Surely the time has come! The sparks from his chariot-wheels of fire just fringe the outline of the Kabyle Hills, and in another minute, before all the Arabs have clambered up and reached their vantage-ground, the whole bay is in a flood of light. The Arabs prostrate themselves before the sun, and "*Allah il Allah*" (God is great) is the burden of their psalm of praise.

But Mahomet's coming is not yet; the Arabs return down the hill, and crowd together to a very different scene. The officers, whom we saw just now leaving the *Place*, have arrived at the Champ de Mars, the drill-ground immediately below us, and here, in the cool morning air, they are exercising and manœuvring troops. There are several companies going through their drill, and the bugle and the drum drown the Muezzins' voices, who, from almost every mosque and turret in the city, repeat their cry to the faithful, " Come to prayers."

THE MOORISH QUARTER.

CHAPTER III.

WE said, in the last chapter, that in Algiers there was very little going on for the visitor or idler ; but if the traveller have anything of the artist in him, he will be delighted with the old town. If he is wise, he will spend the first week in wandering about, and losing himself in the winding streets, going here, there, and every-where on a picturesque tour of inspection. His artistic tendencies will probably lead him to spend much time in the Moorish cafés, where he may sit down unmolested (if unwelcomed) for hours on a mat, and drink his little saucer of thick, sweet coffee, for which he pays one

sou, and smoke in the midst of a group of
silent Moors, who may perchance acknowledge
his presence by a slight gesture, and offer him
their pipes; but who will more frequently affect
not to see him, and sit still doing absolutely
nothing, with that dignified solemnity peculiar
to the East.

He will pass through narrow streets and between mysterious-looking old houses that meet
overhead and shut out the sky; he will jostle
often, in these narrow ways, soft plump objects
in white gauze, whose eyes and ankles give the
only visible signs of humanity; he may turn back
to watch the wonderful dexterity with which a
young Arab girl balances a load of fruit upon
her head down to the market-place; and he will,
if he is not careful, be finally carried down himself by an avalanche of donkeys, — driven by a
negro gamin who sits on the tail of the last, —
threading their way noiselessly and swiftly, and

carrying everything before them;* and he will probably take refuge under the ruined arch of some old mosque, whose graceful lines and rich decoration are still visible here and there; and he will in a few hours be enchanted with the place, and the more so for the reason that we have already hinted at, namely, that in Algiers he is *let alone*, that he is free to wander and "moon" about at will, without custodian or commissionaire, or any of the tribe of "valets de place."

He may go into the Grand Divan; or into the streets where the embroiderers are at work, sitting in front of their open shops, amongst heaps of silks, rich stuffs, and every variety of material; or where the old merchant traders, whose occu-

---

* How different from what we read of in *Æothen*. The cry is not, "Get out of the way, O old man! O virgin! — the Englishman, he comes, he comes!" If we were to push an old man out of the way, or, ever so little, forget our duty to a fair pedestrian, we should be brought up before the Cadi, and fined and scorned by a jury of unbelievers!

pation is nearly gone, sit smoking out their lazy,
uncommercial lives.

, He may go to the old Moorish bath, in a building of curious pattern, which is as well worth
seeing as anything in Algiers; and, if an Arabic
scholar, he may pick up an acquaintance or two
amongst the Moors, and visit their homes when
their wives are away for the day, on some mourn-
ing expedition to a suburban cemetery. He may
explore innumerable crooked, irregular streets,
with low doorways and carved lattices, some
painted, some gilt; the little narrow windows
and the grilles being as perfectly after the old
type as when the Moors held undivided possession of the city.

One old street, now pulled down, we remember
well; it was the one always chosen for an evening stroll, because it faced the western sea, and
caught and reflected from its pavement and from
its white walls the last tints of sunset long after

the cobblers and the tinkers in the lower town
had lighted their little lanterns, and the cafés
were flaring in the French quarter. It was steep
and narrow; so steep, in fact, that steps were
made in the pavement to climb it. Dark at the
lower end, at the upper there was the dome of a
mosque shining in the sun. Like the child's picture of "Jacob's ladder," it was brighter and
more resplendent at each step, ending in a blaze
of gold.

We are often reminded of Spain in these old
streets; there are massive wooden doors studded
with iron bosses or huge nails as we see them
at Toledo, and there is sometimes to be seen over
them the emblem of the human hand pointing
upwards, which recalls the Gate of Justice at the
entrance to the Alhambra at Granada. The
Moors cling to their old traditions, and the belief that they will some day reconquer Spain is
still an article of faith. But if ever the Moors

are to regain their imaginary lost possessions in Spain, they must surely be made of sterner stuff than the present race, who, judging from appearances, are little likely to do anything great.

There are little shops and dark niches where the Moors sit cross-legged, with great gourds and festoons of dried fruits hanging above and around them; the piles of red morocco slippers, the odd-shaped earthenware vessels, and the wonderful medley of form and color, resembling in variety the bazaars at Constantinople, or carrying us in imagination still farther East.

Other sights and sounds we might mention, some not quite so pleasant, but peculiarly Eastern; and we should not forget to note the peculiar scent of herbs and stuffs, which, mingled with the aroma of coffee and tobacco, was sometimes almost overpowering in the little covered streets; and one odor that went up regularly on Sunday

mornings in the Moorish quarter that was not
incense, and which it took us a long time to
discover the origin of, — an Arab branding his
donkeys with his monogram !

Everything we purchase is odd and quaint,
irregular or curious in some way. Every piece
of embroidery, every remnant of old carpet, differs
from another in pattern as the leaves on the
trees. There is no repetition, and herein lies its
charm and true value to us. Every fabric differs
either in pattern or combination of colors, — it
is something, as we said, unique, something to
treasure, something that will not remind us of
the mill.

If we explore still further we shall come to the
Arab quarter, where we also find characteristic
things. Here we may purchase for about thirty
francs a Kabyle match-lock rifle, or an old sabre
with beautifully ornamented hilt; we may, if we
please, ransack piles of primitive and rusty im-

3 *

plements of all kinds, and pick up curious women's ornaments, — beads, coral, and anklets of filagree work ; and, if we are fortunate, meet with a complete set or suit of harness and trappings, once the property of some insolvent Arab chief, and of a pattern made familiar to us in the illustrated history of the Cid.

In the midst of the Moorish quarter, up a little narrow street (reached in five or six minutes from the centre of the town) passing under an archway and between white walls that nearly meet overhead, we come to a low dark door, with a heavy handle and latch which opens and shuts with a crashing sound ; and if we enter the courtyard and ascend a narrow staircase in one corner, we come suddenly upon the interior view of the first or principal floor of our Moorish home.

The house has two stories, and there is also an upper terrace from which we overlook the town. The arrangement of the rooms round the courtyard, all opening inwards, is excellent : they are cool in summer, and warm even on the coldest nights ; and although we are in a noisy and thickly populated part of the town, we are ignorant of what goes on outside, the massive walls keeping out nearly all sound. The floors and walls are tiled, so that they can be cleansed and cooled by water being thrown over them ; the carpets and cushions spread about invite one to the most luxurious repose ; tables and chairs are unknown ; there is nothing to offend the eye in shape or form, nothing to offend the ear, — not even a door to slam.

Above, there is an open terrace, where we sit in the mornings and evenings, and can realize the system of life on the house-tops of the East. Here we can cultivate the vine, grow roses and other flowers, build for ourselves extempore arbors, and live literally in the open air.

From this terrace we overlook the flat roofs of the houses of the Moorish part of the city; and if we peep over, down into the streets immediately below us, a curious hum of sounds comes up. Our neighbors are certainly industrious: they embroider, they make slippers, they hammer at metal work, they break earthenware and mend it, and appear to quarrel all day long, within a few feet of us; but as we sit in the room from which our sketch is taken, the sounds become mingled and subdued into a pleasant tinkle which is almost musical, and which we can, if we please, shut out entirely by dropping a curtain across the doorway.

Our attendants are Moorish, and consist of one old woman, whom we see by accident (closely veiled) about once a month, and a bare-legged, barefooted Arab boy who waits upon us. There are pigeons on the roof, a French poodle that frequents the lower regions, and a guardian of our doorstep who haunts it day and night, whose portrait is given at page 98.

Here we work with the greatest freedom and comfort, without interruption or any drawbacks that we can think of. The climate is so equal, warm, and pleasant, even in December and January, that by preference we generally sit on the upper terrace, where we have the perfection of light, and are at the same time sufficiently protected from sun and wind. At night we sleep almost in the open air, and need scarcely drop the curtains at the arched doorways of our rooms; there are no mosquitoes to trouble us, and there is certainly no fear of intrusion. There is also perfect stillness, for our neighbors are at rest soon after sundown.

Such is a general sketch of our dwelling in Algiers; let us for a moment, by way of contrast, turn in imagination to London, and picture to ourselves our friends as they are working at home. It is considered very desirable, if not essential, to an artist, that his immediate surroundings should be in some sort graceful and harmonious, and it is a lesson worth learning, to see what may be done, with ingenuity and taste, towards converting a single room, in a dingy street, into a fitting abode of the arts.

We know a certain painter well, one whose studio it is always a delight to enter, and whose devotion to Art for its own sake (both music and painting) has always stood in the way of his advancement and pecuniary success. He has converted a room in a dark street in London into a charming nook where color, form, and texture are all considered in the simplest details of decoration, where there is nothing inharmonious to eye or ear, but where perhaps the sound of the guitar may be heard a little too often. The walls of his studio are draped, the light falls softly from above, the doorway is arched, the seats are couches or carpets on a raised daïs, a Florentine lamp hangs from the ceiling, a medley of vases, costumes, old armor, &c., are grouped about in picturesque confusion, and our friend, in an easy undress of the last century, works away in the midst.

Not to particularize further, let the reader consider for a moment what one step beyond his own door brings about, on an average winter's day. A straight, ungraceful, colorless costume of the latter half of the nineteenth century which he *must* assume, a hat of the period, an umbrella raised to keep off sleet and rain, and for landscape a damp, dreary, muddy, blackened street, with a vista of areas and lamp-posts!

Perhaps the most depressing prospect in the world is that from a doorstep in a narrow street in London on a November morning about nine o'clock; but of this enough. We think of our friend as we sit out here on our *terrasse*, — shel-

tering ourselves on the same day, at the same
hour, from the sun's rays, — we think of him
painting Italian scenes by the light of his gas
"sun-burner," and wish he would come out to
Algiers. "Surely," we would say to him, "it is
something gained, if we can, ever so little, harmonize the realities of life with our ideal world;
if we can, without remark, dress ourselves more
as we dress our models, and so live, that one
step from the studio to the street shall not be
the abomination of desolation." *

Let us turn again to Nature and to Light, and
transport the reader to a little white house over-
looking a beautiful city on the North African
shore, where summer is perpetual and indoor life
the exception; and draw a picture for him which
should be fascinating, and which certainly is true.

* It would be obviously in bad taste for Europeans to walk
in the streets of Algiers, *en costume Maure;* but we may
make considerable modifications in our attire in an Oriental
city, to our great comfort and peace of mind.

ALGIERS, *Sunrise*, December 10.

The mysterious, indefinable charm of the first break of day is an old and favorite theme in all countries and climates, and one on which perhaps little that is new can be said. In the East it is always striking, but in Algiers it seems to us peculiarly so ; for sleeping, or more often lying awake, with the clear crisp night air upon our faces, it comes to our couch in the dreamiest way imaginable, — instead of being clothed (as poets express it) with the veil of night, a mantle seems rather to be spread over us in the morning ; there is perfect quiet at this hour, and we seem to be almost under a spell not to disturb the stillness, — the dawn whispers to us so softly and soothingly that we are powerless to do aught but watch or sleep.

The break of day is perhaps first announced to us by a faint stream of light across the courtyard, or the dim shadow of a marble pillar on

E

the wall. In a few minutes we hear the distant barking of a dog, a slight rustle in the pigeon-house above, or a solitary cry from a minaret which tells us that the city is awaking. We rouse ourselves and steal out quietly to the upper terrace to see a sight of sights, — one of those things that books tell us, rightly or wrongly, is alone worth coming to Algeria to see.

The canopy of stars, that had encompassed us so closely during the night, as if to shut in the courtyard overhead, seems lifted again, and the stars themselves are disappearing fast in the gray expanse of sky; and as we endeavor to trace them, looking intently seaward, towards the north and east, we can just discern an horizon line and faint shadows of the "sleeping giants," that we know to be not far off. Soon — in about the same time that it takes to write these lines — they begin to take form and out-

line one by one, a tinge of delicate pearly pink
is seen at intervals through their shadows, and
before any nearer objects have come into view,
the whole coast line and the mountains of Kabylia, stretching far to the eastward, are flushed
with rosy light, opposed to a veil of twilight
gray which is spread over the city.

Another minute or two, and our shadows are
thrown sharply on a glowing wall, towers and
domes come distinctly into view, house-tops innumerable range themselves in close array at our
feet, and we, who but a few minutes ago seemed
to be standing as it were alone upon the top of
a high mountain, are suddenly and closely be-
leaguered. A city of flat white roofs, towers,
and cupolas, relieved here and there by colored
awnings, green shutters, and dark doorways, and
by little courtyards blooming with orange and
citron trees, intersected with innumerable winding ways, which look like streams forcing their

way through a chalk-cliff, has all grown up before our eyes; and beyond it, seaward, a harbor,
and a fleet of little vessels with their white
sails, are seen shining in the sun.

Then come the hundred sounds of a waking
city, mingling and increasing every moment; and
the flat roofs (some so close that we can step upon
them) are soon alive with those quaint white
figures we meet in the streets, passing to and fro,
from roof to roof, apparently without restraint
or fear. There are numbers of children peeping
out from odd corners and loop-holes, and women
with them, some dressed much less scrupulously
than we see them in the market-place, and some,
to tell the truth, entirely without the white
robes aforesaid. A few, a very few, are already
winding their way through the streets to the
nearest mosque, but the majority are collected in
groups in conversation, enjoying the sweet sea-
breeze, which comes laden with the perfume of

orange-trees, and a peculiar delicious scent as of violets.

The pigeons on the roof-tops now plume their gilded wings, and soar — not upward, but downward, far away into space ; they scarcely break the silence in the air, or spread their wings as they speed along.

O, what a flight above the azure sea !

"Quis dabat mihi pennas sicut columbæ" ;

. . . . .

for the very action of flying seems repose to them.

It is still barely sunrise on this soft December morning, the day's labor has scarcely begun, the calm is so perfect that existence alone seems a delight, and the Eastern aroma, if we may so express it, that pervades the air might almost lull us to sleep again, but Allah wills it otherwise.

Suddenly — with terrible impulse and shrill

accent impossible to describe — a hurricane of
women's voices succeeds the calm. Is it treach-
ery? Is it scandal? Has Hassan proved faith-
less, or has Fatima fled? O the screeching and
yelling that succeeded to the quiet beauty of the
morning! O the rushing about of veiled (now
all closely veiled) figures on house-tops! O the
weeping and wailing, and literal, terrible gnash-
ing of teeth! "Tell it not upon the house-tops,"
(shall we ever forget it being told on the house-
tops?) "let not a whole city know thy misdeeds,"
is written in the Koran; "it is better for the
faithful to come to prayers!" Merciful powers!
how the tempest raged until the sun was up and
the city was alive again, and its sounds helped to
drown the clamor!

Let us come down, for our Arab boy now
claps his hands in sign that (on a little low table
or tray, six inches from the ground) coffee and
pipes are provided for the unbelievers; and like

the Calendar in Eastern story, he proceeds to tell us the cause of the tumult, — a trinket taken from one wife and given to another! O Islam! that a lost bracelet or a jealous wife should make the earth tremble so!

MODELS.

CHAPTER IV.

" MODELS."

FROM the roof-tops of our own and the neighboring houses we have altogether many opportunities of sketching, and making studies from life. By degrees, by fits and starts, and by most uncertain means (such as attracting curiosity, making little presents, &c.), we manage to scrape up a distant talking acquaintance with some of the mysterious, wayward creatures we have spoken of, and, in short, to become almost "neighborly."

But we never get much nearer than talking distance, conversing from one roof to another with a narrow street like a river flowing between

4

us; and only once or twice during our winter
sojourn did we succeed in enticing a veiled houri
to venture on our terrace and shake hands with
the "Frank." If we could manage to hold a young
lady in conversation, and exhibit sufficient ad-
miration of her to induce her, ever so slightly,
to unveil whilst we made a hasty sketch, it was
about all that we could fairly succeed in accom-
plishing, and "the game was hardly worth the
candle"; it took, perhaps, an hour to ensnare our
bird, and in ten minutes or less she would be
again on the wing. Veiled beauties are interesting, sometimes much more interesting for being
veiled; but it does not serve our artistic pur-
poses much to see two splendid black eyes and a
few white robes.

However, models we must have, although the
profession is almost unknown in Algiers. At
Naples we have only to go down to the seashore, at Rome to the steps of St. Peter's, and

we find "subjects" enough, who will come for
the asking ; but here, where there is so much
distinctive costume and variety of race, French
artists seem to make little use of their opportunities.

It takes some days before we can hear of any
one who will be willing to sit for double the
usual remuneration. But they come at last, and
when it gets abroad that the Franks have money
and "mean business," we have a number of ap-
plicants, some of whom are not very desirable, *
and none particularly attractive. We select
"Fatima" first, because she is the youngest and
has the best costume, and also because she comes
with her father and appears tractable. She is
engaged at two francs an hour, which she con-
siders poor pay.

How shall we give the reader an idea of this
little creature, when she comes next morning and
coils herself up amongst the cushions in the cor-

ner of our room, like a young panther in the Jardin des Plantes? Her costume, when she throws off her haïk (and with it a tradition of the Mohammedan faith, that forbids her to show her face to an unbeliever), is a rich loose crimson jacket embroidered with gold, a thin white bodice, loose silk trousers reaching to the knee and fastened round the waist by a magnificent sash of various colors, red morocco slippers, a profusion of rings on her little fingers, and bracelets and anklets of gold filagree work. Through her waving black hair are twined strings of coins and the folds of a silk handkerchief, the hair falling at the back in plaits below the waist.

She is not beautiful, she is scarcely interesting in expression, and she is decidedly unsteady. She seems to have no more power of keeping herself in one position or of remaining in one part of the room, or even of being quiet, than a

humming-top. The whole thing is an unuttera-
ble bore to her, for she does not even reap the
reward, — her father or husband or male attend-
ant always taking the money.

She is *petite*, constitutionally phlegmatic, and
as fat as her parents can manage to make her;
she has small hands and feet, large rolling eyes,
— the latter made to appear artificially large by
the application of henna or antimony black; her
attitudes are not ungraceful, but there is a want
of character about her, and an utter abandonment
to the situation, peculiar to all her race. In short,
her movements are more suggestive of a little
caged animal that had better be petted and
caressed, or kept at a safe distance, according to
her humor. She does one thing, — she smokes
incessantly, and makes cigarettes with a skill and
rapidity which are wonderful.

Her age is thirteen, and she has been married
six months; her ideas appear to be limited to

three or four, and her pleasures, poor creature! are equally circumscribed. She had scarcely ever left her father's house, and had never spoken to a man until her marriage. No wonder that we, in spite of a little Arabic on which we prided ourselves, could not make much way; no wonder that we came very rapidly to the conclusion that the houris of the Arabian Nights must have been dull creatures, and their "Entertainments" rather a failure, if there were no diviner fire than this. No wonder that the Moors advocate a plurality of wives; for if one represents an emotion, a harem would scarcely suffice.

We get on but indifferently with our studies with this young lady, and, to tell the truth, not too well in Fatima's good graces. Our opportunities are not great, our command of Arabic is limited, and, indeed, we do not feel particularly inspired. We cannot tell her many love-stories, or sing songs set to a "*tom-tom*"; we can, indeed,

offer " backshish " in the shape of tobacco and
sweetmeats, or some trifling European ornament
or trinket; but it is clear that she would prefer a
greater amount of familiarity, and more demon-
strative tokens of esteem. However, she came
several times, and we succeeded in obtaining
some valuable studies of color, and " bits," memo-
randa only; but very useful, from being taken
down almost unconsciously, in such a luminous
key, and with a variety of reflected light and
pure shadow tone, that we find unapproachable
in after work.

As for sketches of character, we obtained very
few of Mauresques; our subjects were, as a rule,
much too restless, and we had one or two "scenes"
before we parted. On one unfortunate occasion
our model insisted upon examining our work
before leaving, and the scorn and contempt
with which it was regarded was anything but
flattering. It nearly caused a breach between

us, for, as she observed, it was not only con-
trary to her creed to have her likeness taken,
but it would be perdition to be thus represented
amongst the Franks.* We promised to be as
careful of this portrait as if it were the original,
and, in fact, said anything to be polite and
soothing.

On another occasion we had been working on
rather more quietly than usual for half an hour,
and were really getting a satisfactory study of a
new position, when, without apparent cause or
warning of any kind, the strange, pale, passion-
less face, which stared like a wooden marionette,
suddenly suffused with crimson, the great eyes
filled with tears, the whole frame throbbed con-
vulsively, and the little creature fell into such a
passion of crying that we were fain to put by

* For fear of the "evil eye." There is a strong belief
amongst Mohammedans that portraits are part of their iden-
tity; and that the original will suffer if the portrait receive
any indignity.

our work and question ourselves whether we had
been cruel or unkind. But it was nothing : the
cup of boredom had been filled to the brim, all
other artifices had failed her to obtain relief from
restraint, and so this apparently lethargic little
being, who had, it seemed, both passion and grief
at command, opened the flood-gates upon us, and
of course gained her end. There was no more
work that day, and she got off with a double
allowance of bonbons, and something like a rec-
onciliation. She gave us her little white hand
at parting, — the fingers and thumbs crowded
with rings, and the nails stained black with
henna, — but the action meant nothing ; we dared
not press it, it was too soft and frail, and the
rings would have cut her fingers ; we could only
hand it tenderly back again, and bid our " model "
farewell.

We got on better afterwards with a Moorish
Jewess, who, for a " consideration," unearthed her

4 * F

property,* including a tiara of gold and jewels, and a bodice of silver embroidery worked on crimson velvet; we purposely reverse the usual position and speak of the embroidery first, because the velvet was almost hidden. She came slouching in one morning, closely wrapped in a dirty shawl, her black hair all dishevelled and half covering her handsome face, her feet bare and her general appearance so much more suggestive of one of the "finest pisantry in the world," that we began to feel doubtful, and to think with Beau Brummel that this must be "one of our failures." But when her mother had arranged the tiara in her hair, when the curtain was drawn aside and the full splendor of the Jewish costume was displayed, — when, in short, the dignity and grace of a queen were before us, we felt rewarded.

* Many of the poorest Jewesses possess gold ornaments as heirlooms, burying them in the ground for security when not in use.

The Jewish dress differs from the Mauresque entirely; it is European in shape, with high waist and flowing robes without sleeves, a square-cut bodice, generally of the same material as the robe itself, and a profusion of gold ornaments, armlets, necklaces, and rings. A pair of tiny velvet slippers (also embroidered) on tiny feet complete the costume, which varies in color, but is generally of crimson or dark velvet.

As a "model," although almost her first appearance in that character, this Jewish woman was very valuable, and we had little trouble, after the first interview, in making her understand our wishes. But we had to pay more than in England; there were many drawbacks, and of course much waste of time. On some holydays and on all Jewish festivals she did not make her appearance, and seemed to think nothing of it when some feast that lasted a week left us stranded with half-done work.

Without being learned in modern *costumes des dames*, we believe we may say that the shape and cut of some of these dresses and the patterns of the embroidery (old as they are) might be copied with advantage by Parisian modistes; and the more we study these old patterns, the more we regret that the *Deœ ex machinâ*, the arbiters of fashion in the city where Fashion is Queen, have not managed to infuse into the costume of the time more character and purity of design, — conditions not inconsistent with splendor, and affording scope, if need be, for any amount of extravagance. We are led irresistibly into this digression, if it be a digression, because the statuesque figure before us displays so many lines of grace and beauty that have the additional charm of novelty. We know, for instance, that the pattern of this embroidery is unique, that the artificer of that curiously twined chain of gold has been dead for ages, that the rings on her fingers and the coins suspended from her hair are many of them real art treasures.*

The result of our studies, as far as regards Moorish women, we must admit to have been, after all, rather limited and unsatisfactory. We never once lighted upon a Moorish face that moved us much by its beauty, for the simple reason that it nearly always lacked expression; anything like emotion seemed inharmonious and out of place, and to disturb the uniformity of its lines. Even those dark lustrous eyes, when lighted by passion, had more of the tiger in them than the tragedy queen.

The perfection of beauty, according to the Moorish ideal, seems to depend principally upon

* The "jewels" turned out to be paste on close inspection, but the gold filagree work and the other ornaments were old, and some very valuable and rare.

symmetry of feature, and is nothing without roundness of limb and a certain flabbiness of texture. It is an ideal of repose, not to say of dulness and insipidity; a heavy type of beauty of which we obtain some idea in a fine drawing, of a young girl, about thirteen years old. The drawing is by a Frenchman, and pretends to no particular artistic excellence, but it attempts to render (and we think succeeds in rendering) the style of a Mohammedan beauty in bridal array; one who is about to fulfil her destiny, and who appears to have as little animation or intelligence as the Prophet ordained for her, being perfectly fitted, according to the Koran, to fill her place in this world and in the next.* Thus decked with her brightest

* It detracts a little from the romance of these things to learn from Mrs. Evans (who witnessed, what only ladies, of course, could witness, the robing and decorating of the bride before marriage) the manner in which the face of a Moorish lady is prepared on the day of marriage.

"An old woman, having carefully washed the bride's face

jewels and adorned with a crown of gold, she waits to meet her lord, to be his "light of the harem," his "sun and moon." What if we, with our refined æsthetic tastes, what if disinterested spectators, vote her altogether the dullest and most uninteresting of beings? what if she seem to us more like some young animal, magnificently harnessed, waiting to be trotted out to the highest bidder? She shakes the coins and beads on her head sometimes, with a slight impatient gesture, and takes chocolate from her little sister, and is petted and pacified just as we should soothe and pacify an impatient steed;

with water, proceeded to whiten it all over with a milky looking preparation, and after touching up the cheeks with rouge (and her eyes with antimony black), bound an amulet round the head; then with a fine camel-hair pencil she passed a line of liquid glue over the eyebrows, and taking from a folded paper a strip of gold-leaf, fixed it across them both, forming one long gilt bar; and then proceeded to give a few finishing touches to the poor lay figure before her by fastening two or three tiny gold spangles on the forehead!"

there is clearly no other way to treat her, it is the will of Allah that she should be so debased ! *

One day we had up a tinker, an old brown grizzled Maltese, who with his implements of trade, his patchwork garments and his dirt, had a tone about him, like a figure from one of the old Dutch masters.   He sat down in the corner of our courtyard against a marble pillar, and made himself quite at home ; he worked with his feet as well as his hands at his grinding ; he chattered, he sang, and altogether made such a clatter that we shall not be likely to forget him.

This gentleman, and the old negro that lived

* We have before spoken of the humanizing influence of beautiful forms and harmony in color in our homes and surroundings ; and we feel acutely that the picture of this Moorish woman, intellectually, does not prove our case ; but Mahomet decreed that women should endeavor to *be* beautiful rather than appreciate or enjoy it.

upon our doorstep, were almost the only subjects that we succeeded in inducing to come
within doors; our other life studies were made
under less favorable circumstances. From the
roof of our own house, it is true, we obtained a
variety of sketches, not, as might be supposed
from the illustrations and pictures with which
all are familiar, of young ladies attired as scantily
as the nymphs at the *Théâtre du Chatelet* in
Paris, standing in pensive attitudes on their
house-tops, but generally of groups of veiled
women, old, ugly, haggard, shrill of voice, and
sometimes rather fierce of aspect, performing
various household duties on the roof-tops, including the beating of carpets and of children,
the carrying of water-pots, and the saying of
prayers.

A chapter on " Models" would not be complete without some mention of the camels, of
which there are numbers to be found in the

Arab quarter of the town. Some of them are splendid creatures, and as different from any exotic specimens that we can see in this country as an acclimatized palm-tree from its wild growth.

Some one tells us that these Algerian "ships of the desert" have not the same sailing qualities, nor the same breadth of beam, as those at Cairo. But (if true) we should have to go to Cairo to study them, so let us be content. We should like to see one or two of our popular artists, who persist in painting camels and desert scenes without ever having been to the East, just sit down here quietly for one day and paint a camel's head; not flinching from the work, but mastering the wonderful texture and shagginess of his thick coat or mane, its massive beauty, and its infinite gradations of color. Such a sitter no portrait-painter ever had in England. Feed him up first, get a boy to keep the flies

A PORTRAIT.

from him, and he will sit almost immovably through the day. He will put on a sad expression in the morning, which will not change; he will give no trouble whatever; he will but sit still and croak.

Do we seem to exaggerate the value of such studies? We cannot exaggerate, if we take into full account the vigorous quality which we impart into our work. And we cannot, perhaps, better illustrate our argument in favor of drawing from what we should call *natural* models, than by comparing the merits of two of the most popular pictures of our time, namely, Frith's "*Derby Day*" and Rosa Bonheur's "*Horse Fair*"; the former pleasing the eye by its cleverness and prettiness, the latter impressing the spectator by its power, and its truthful rendering of animal life. The difference between the two painters is probably one more of education than of natural gifts. But whilst the style of

the former is grafted on a fashion, the latter is
founded on a rock, — the result of a close study
of nature, chastened by classic feeling, and a
remembrance, it may be, of the friezes of the
Parthenon.

OUR "LIFE SCHOOL."

CHAPTER V.

OUR "LIFE SCHOOL."

OF the various studies to be made in Algiers, there are none so characteristic as the Moors in their homes, seated at their own doors or benches at work, or at the numerous cafés and bazaars; and nothing seems to harmonize so well in these Moorish streets as the groups of natives, both Moors and negroes, with their bright costumes, and wares for sale. Color and contrast of color seem to be considered, or *felt*, everywhere. Thus, for instance, no two Orientals will walk down a street side by side, unless the colors of their costume harmonize or blend together (they seem to know it instinctively); and then there is always gray or some quiet contrasting tone for a background, and a sky of deep blue. A negress will generally be found selling oranges or citrons; an Arab boy, with a red fez and white turban, carrying purple fruit in a basket of leaves; and so on. The reader will think this fanciful, but it is truer than he imagines; let him come and see.

It was not at all times easy to sketch in the open street, on account of the curiosity it excited; a crowd collecting sometimes until it became almost impossible to breathe. The plan was to go as often as possible to the cafés and divans, and by degrees to make friends with the Moors.

There was one café, in a street that we have been to so often that it is as familiar to us as any in the Western world, where by dint of a little tact and a small outlay of tobacco we managed to make ourselves quite at home, and were permitted to work away all day comparatively unmolested. It was a narrow and steep overhanging street, crowded at all times with Moors on one side embroidering, or pretending to sell goods of various kinds ; and on the opposite side there was a café, not four feet distant, where a row of about eighteen others sat and smoked, and contemplated their brethren at work. The street was full of traffic, being an important thorough-fare from the upper to the lower town, and there were perpetually passing up and down droves of laden donkeys, men with burdens carried on poles between them, venders of fruit, bread, and live fowls, and crowds of people of every denomination.

In a little corner out of sight, where we were certainly rather closely packed, we used to install ourselves continually and sketch the people passing to and fro. The Moors in the café used to sit beside us all day, and watch and *wait ;* they gave us a grave, silent salutation when we took our places, and another when we left, but we never got much further with our unknown neighbors. If we can imagine a coterie in a small political club, where the open discussion of politics is, with one consent, tabooed for fear of a disturbance, and where the most frolicsome of its members play at chess for relaxation, we shall get some notion of the state of absolute decorum which existed in our little *café maure.*

It was very quaint. The memory of the grave, quiet faces of these polite Moorish gentlemen, looking so smooth and clean in their white bournouses, seated solemnly doing nothing, haunts us to this day. Years elapsed between our first and last visit to our favorite street; yet there they were when we came again, still doing nothing in a row; and opposite to them the merchants who do no trade, also sitting in their accustomed places, surrounded with the same old wares. There was the same old negro in a dark corner making coffee, and handing it to the same customers, sitting in the same places, in the same dream.

There is certainly both art and mystery in doing nothing well, which these men achieve in
their peculiar lives; here they sit for years together, silently waiting, without a trace of boredom on their faces, and without exhibiting a
gesture of impatience. They — the " gentlemen "
in the café on the right hand — have saved up
money enough to keep life together; they have
forever renounced work, and can look on with
complacency at their poorer brethren. They have
their traditions, their faith, their romance of life,
and the curious belief before alluded to, that if
they fear God and Mahomet, and sit here long
enough, they will one day be sent for to Spain,
to repeople the houses where their fathers dwelt.
This corner is the one *par excellence* where the
Moors sit and wait. There is the " wall of wailing " at Jerusalem; there is the " street of waiting " in Algiers, where the Moors sit clothed in
white, dreaming of heaven, with an aspect of

more than content, in a state of dreamy delight,
— achieved, apparently, more by habit of mind
than any opiates, — the realization of "*Keyf.*"

Not far from this street, but still in the Moorish quarter, we may witness a much more ani-
mated scene, and obtain in some respects a better
study of character and costume, — at a clothes auction in the neighborhood of the principal bazaar.
If we go in the afternoon, we shall probably find
a crowd collected in a courtyard, round a number
of Jews who are selling clothes, silks, and stuffs;
and so intent are they all on the business that
is going forward, that we are able to take up a
good position to watch the proceedings.

We arrived one day at this spot just as a terrible scuffle or wrangle was going forward between
ten or a dozen old men, surrounded by at least a
hundred spectators, about the quality or owner-
ship of some garment. The merits of the discussion were of little interest to us, and were

probably of little importance to anybody, but the result was a spectacle that we could never have imagined, and certainly could never have seen, in any other land.

This old garment had magical powers, and was a treasure to *us* at least. It attracted the old and young, the wise and foolish, the excited combatant and the calm and dignified spectator; it collected them all in a large square courtyard with plain whitewashed walls and Moorish arcades. On one side a palm-tree drooped its gigantic leaves, and cast broad shadows on the ground, which in some places was almost of the brightness of orange; on the other side, half in sunlight, half in shadow, a heavy awning was spread over a raised daïs or stage, and through its tatters and through the deep arcades the sky appeared in patches of the deepest blue, — blue of a depth and brilliancy that few painters have ever succeeded in depicting. It gave in a wider and

truer sense just that quality to our picture — if
we may be excused a little technicality and a
familiar illustration — that a broad red sash
thrown across the bed of a sleeping child in
Millais's picture in the Royal Academy Exhibition
of 1867, gave to his composition, as many readers
may remember.

But we cannot take our eyes from the principal
group, or do much more than watch the crowd in
its changing phases. To give any idea of the up-
roar — the "row," we ought to call it — would
be to weary the reader with a polyglot of words
and sentences, some not too choice, and many too
shrill and fiercely accentuated; but to picture
the general aspect in a few words is worth a
trial, although to do this we must join the throng
and fight our way to the front.

Where have we seen the like? We have seen
such upturned faces in pictures of the early days
of the Reformation by Henry Leys; we have

seen such passion in *Shylock*, such despair in *Lear*, such grave and imposing-looking men with "reverend beards" in many pictures by the old masters; but seldom have we seen such concentration of emotion (if we may so express it) and unity of purpose in one group.

Do our figure-painters want a subject, with variety of color and character in one canvas? They need not go to the bazaars of Constantinople, or to the markets of the East. Let them follow us here, crushing close to the platform, our faces nearly on a level with the boards. Look at the colors, at the folds of their cloaks, bournouses, and yachmahs, — purple, deep red, and spotless white, all crushed together, — with their rich transparent shadows, as the sun streams across them, reflected from the walls; whilst the heavy awning throws a curious glow over the figures, and sometimes almost conceals their features with a dazzle of reflected light. Look at the legs of

these eager traders, as they struggle and fight and
stand on tiptoe to catch a glimpse of some new
thing exposed for sale ; look at them well, — the
lean, the shambling, the vigorous, the bare bronze
(bronzed with sun and grime), the dark hose,
the purple silk, and the white cotton, the latter
the special affectation of the dandy Jew. What
a medley, but what character here! the group
from knee to ankle forms a picture alone. And
thus they crowd together for half an hour, whilst
all ordinary business seems suspended. Nothing
could be done with such a clatter, not to mention
the heat. O, how the Arab gutturals, the impossible consonants (quite impossible to unprac-
tised European lips), were interjected and hurled,
so to speak, to and fro! How much was said
to no purpose, how incoherent it all seemed, and
how we wished for a few vowels to cool the air!

In half an hour a calm has set in, and the
steady business of the day is allowed to go for-

ward; we may now smoke our pipes in peace, and from a quiet corner watch the proceedings almost unobserved, asking ourselves a question or two suggested by the foregoing scene. Is expression really worth anything? Is the exhibition of passion much more than acting? Shall gray beards and flowing robes carry dignity with them any more, if a haggle about old clothes can produce it in five minutes?

Here we sit and watch for hours, wondering at the apparently endless variety of the patterns and colors of the fabrics exposed for sale; and — perhaps we dose, perhaps we dream. Is it the effect of the hachshish? Is it the strong coffee? Are we indeed dreaming, or is the auction a sham? Surely that pretty bright handkerchief — now held up and eagerly scanned by bleared old eyes, now crumpled and drawn sharply between haggard fingers — is an old friend, and has no business in a sale like this! Let us rub our eyes and try and remember where we have seen it before. Yes, — there is no mistaking the pattern, — we have seen it in Spain. It was bound turbanwise round the head of a woman who performed in the bull-ring at Seville, on the occasion of a particularly high and rollicking festival of the "Catholic Church"; it was handed out of a diligence window one dark night on the Sierra Morena, when a mule had broken its leg, and the only method of getting it along was to tie the injured limb to the girth, and let the animal hop on three legs for the rest of the way; it found its way into the Tyrol, worn as a sash; it was in the market-place at Bastia in Corsica, in the hands of a maiden selling fruit; it flaunted at Marseilles, drying in the wind on a ship's spar; and the last time we saw it, if our memory serves us well, it was carefully taken from a drawer in a little shop, "*Au Dey d'Alger*," in the Rue de Rivoli in Paris, and offered to us by that greatest of all humbugs, Mustapha, as the latest Algerian thing in neckties, which he asked fifteen francs for, and would gladly part with for three.

It was a pattern we knew by heart, that we meet with in all parts of the world, thanks to the universality of Manchester cottons. But the pattern was simple and good, nothing but an arrangement of red and black stripes on a maize ground, and therein lay its success. It had its origin in the first principles of decoration, it trangressed no law or canon of taste, it was easily and cheaply made (as all the best patterns are), and so it travelled round the world, and the imitation work came to be sold in, perhaps, the very bazaar whence the pattern first came, and its originators squabbled over the possession of it as of something unique.

But we can hardly regret the repetition of these Moorish patterns, for they are useful in such

a variety of ways. Wind one of the handker-
chiefs in and out amongst dark tresses, and see
what richness it gives; make a turban of it for
a negress's head; tie it nattily under the chin
of a little Parisienne, and, *hey presto* — she is
pretty! make a sash of it, or throw it loosely
on the ground, and the effect is graceful and
charming to the eye. In some Japanese and
Chinese materials we may meet with more brilliant achievements in positive colors; but the
Moors seem to excel all other nations in taste,
and in their skilful juxtaposition of tints. We
have seen a Moorish designer hard at work, with
a box of butterflies' wings for his school of design,
and we might, perhaps, take the hint at home.

But we must leave the Moors and their beautiful fabrics for a while, and glance at the Arab
quarter of the town. We shall see the latter
by and by in the plains and in their tents in
their traditionary aspect; but here we come in

contact with a somewhat renegade and disreputable race, who hang, as it were, on the outskirts of civilization. Many of them have come from the neighboring villages and from their camps across the plains of the Sahel, and have set up a market of their own, where they are in full activity, trading with each other and with the Frank.* Here they may be seen by hundreds, — some buying and selling, some fighting, and not unfrequently cursing one another heartily; others ranged close together in rows upon the ground, like so many white loaves ready for baking. Calm they are, and almost dignified in appearance, when sitting smoking in conclave; but only give them something to quarrel about, touch them up ever so little on their irritable side, and they will beat Geneva washerwomen for clatter.

---

* This market-place is a sort of commercial neutral ground, where both Arabs and Kabyles meet the French in the strictest amity, and cheat them if they can.

Take them individually, these trading men, who
have had years of intercourse with their French
conquerors, and they disappoint us altogether.
They are no longer true followers of the Prophet,
although they are a great obstruction to traffic
by spreading carpets on the ground in the middle of the road, and prostrating themselves towards Mahomet and the sun. Trade — paltry,
mean, and cowardly as it makes men — has done
the Arab irreparable harm : it has taught him to
believe in counterfeits and little swindles as a
legitimate mode of life, to pass bad money, and
to cringe to a conqueror because he could make
money thereby. He could not do these things
in the old days, with his face to the sun.

The Arab is generally pictured to us in his tent
or with his tribe, calm, dignified, and brave, and
perhaps we may meet with him thus on the other
side of the Sahel; but here in Algiers he is a
metamorphosed creature. The camels that crouch

upon the ground, and scream and bite at passers-
by, are more dignified and consistent in their
ill-tempered generation than these "Sons of the
Prophet," these "Lights of Truth."

And they have actually caught European tricks.
What shall we say when two Arabs meet in the
street, and after a few words interchanged, pass
away from each other with a quickened, jaunty
step, like two city men, who have "lost time,"
and must make it up by a spurt! Shall we respect our noble Arab any more when we see him
walking abroad with a stereotyped, plausible smile
upon his face, every action indicating an eye to
the main chance?*

* It may seem a stretch of fancy, but even the bournous
itself, with its classic outline and flowing folds, loses half
its dignity and picturesqueness on these men. It has been
rather vulgarized of late years in Western Europe; and
when we see it carried on the arm of an Arab (as we do
sometimes), there is a suggestion of opera stalls, and lingering last good-nights on unromantic doorsteps, that is fatal to
its patriarchal character.

A step lower, of which there are too many examples in the crowd, and there is a sadder metamorphose yet, — the patriarch turned scamp; one who has left his family and his tribe to seek his fortune. Look at him, with his ragged bournous, his dirt, and his cringing ways, and contrast his life now with what he has voluntarily abandoned. O, how civilization has lowered him in his own eyes; how his courage has turned to bravado and his tact to cunning; how even natural affection has languished, and family ties are but threads of the lightest tissue! He has failed in his endeavor to trade, he has disobeyed the Koran, and is an outcast and unclean, — one of the waifs and strays of cities!

As we wend our way homeward, as John Bunyan says, "thinking of these things," we see two tall white figures go down to the water side, like the monks in Millais's picture of "A Dream of the Past." They bow their heads by the seashore, in the evening light, and their reflections are repeated in the water. It is the hour of prayer; what are they doing? They are fishing with a modern rod and line, and their little floats are painted with the tricolor.

H

ALOES AND PALMS.

CHAPTER VI.

THE BOUZAREAH. — A STORM.

I T would be passing over the most enjoyable part of our life abroad, if we omitted all mention of those delightful days spent on the hillsides of Mustapha, on the heights of the Bouzareah, and indeed everywhere in the neighborhood of Algiers, sketching in winter time in the open air.

Odors of orange-groves, the aromatic scent of cedars, the sweet breath of wild flowers, roses, honeysuckles, and violets, should pervade this page; something should be done, which no words can accomplish, to give the true impression of the scene, to picture the luxuriant growth of vege-

tation, radiant in a sunshine which to a North-
erner is unknown ; to realize in any method of
description the sense of calm enjoyment of living this pure life in a climate neither too hot
nor too cold, neither too enervating nor too
exciting, of watching the serene days decline
into sunsets that light the Kabyle Hills with
crests of gold, and end in sudden twilights that
spread a weird unearthly light across the silver
sea.

We take our knapsacks and walk off merrily
enough on the bright December mornings, often
before the morning gun has fired or the city is
fully awake.   If we go out at the eastern gate
and keep along near the seashore in the direction
of the *Maison Carrée* (a French fort, now used
as a prison), we obtain fine views of the bay, and
of the town of Algiers itself, with its mole and
harbor stretching out far into the sea.   There is
plenty to interest us here, if it is only in sketch-

ing the wild palmettos, or in watching the half-
wild Arabs who camp in the neighborhood, and
build mud huts which they affect to call cafés,
and where we can, if we please, obtain rest and
shelter from the midday sun, and a considerable amount of "stuffiness" for one sou. But
there is no need to trouble them, as there are
plenty of shady valleys and cactus-hedges to
keep off the sun's rays; the only disturbers of
our peace are the dogs who guard the Arab en-
campments, and have to be diligently kept off
with stones.

Perhaps the best spots for quiet work are the
precincts of the Marabouts' tombs, where we can
take refuge unobserved behind some old wall, and
return quietly to the same spot day after day.
And here, as one experience of sketching from
Nature, let us allude to the theory (laid down
pretty confidently by those who have never reduced it to practice), that one great advantage of

this climate is, that you may work at the same sketch from day to day, and continue it where you left off! You can do nothing of the kind. If your drawing is worth anything, it will at least have recorded something of the varying phases of light and shade that really alter every hour.

Let us take an example. About six feet from us, at eight o'clock in the morning, the sheer white wall of a Moslem tomb is glowing with a white heat, and across it are cast the shadows of three palm-leaves, which at a little distance have the contrasted effect of the blackness of night.* Approach a little nearer and examine the real color of these photographic leaf-lines, shade off, with the hand, as much as possible of the wall, the sky, and the reflected light from

* Under some conditions of the atmosphere we have obtained more perfect outlines of the leaves of the aloe, with their curiously indented edges and spear-points, *from their shadows* rather than from the leaves themselves.

surrounding leaves, and these dark shadows become a delicate pearl-gray, deepening into mauve,
or partaking sometimes of the tints of the rich
earth below them. They will be deeper yet before noon, and pale again, and uncertain and
fantastic in shape, before sundown. If we sketch
these shadows only each hour, as they pass from
left to right upon the wall (laying down a different wash for the ground each time), and place
them side by side in our note-book, we shall
have made some discoveries in light and transparent shadow tone which will be very valuable
in after time. No two days or two hours are
under precisely the same atmospheric conditions;
the gradations and changes are extraordinary, and
would scarcely be believed in by any one who
had not watched them.

Thus, although we cannot continue a sketch
once left off, to any purpose, we may obtain an
infinite and overwhelming variety of work in one

day, in the space of a few yards by the side of some old well or Marabout's tomb.

We seldom returned from a day in the country without putting up for an hour or two at one of the numerous cafés, or caravanserai, built near some celebrated spring, with seats placed invitingly by the roadside, under the shade of trees. There were generally a number of Arabs and French soldiers collected in the middle of the day, drinking coffee, playing at dominoes, or taking a siesta on the mats under the cool arcades, and often some Arab musicians, who hummed and droned monotonous airs ; there were always plenty of beggars to improve the occasion, and perhaps a group of half-naked boys, who would get up an imitation of the " Beni Zouzoug Arabs," and go through hideous contortions, inflicting all kinds of torments on each other for a few sous. It is pleasant to put up at one of these cafés during the heat of the day, and to be able to walk

in and take our places quietly amongst the Arabs
and Moors, without any particular notice or remark; and delightful (O, how delightful!) to yield
to the combined influences of the coffee, the hachshish, the tom-tom, and the heat, and fall asleep
and dream,—dream that the world is standing
still, that politics and Fenianism are things of
the past, and that all the people in a hurry are
dead. Pleasant, and not a
little perplexing too, when
waking, for the eye to rest
on the delicate outline of a
little window in the wall
above, which, with its spiral
columns and graceful pro-
portions, seems the very
counterpart in miniature of
some Gothic cathedral screen. If we examine
it, it is old and Moorish (these buildings date
back several hundred years), and yet so perfect

6

is its similarity to later work, that our ideas on orders of architecture become confused and vague. We may not attempt to discover the cause of the similarity, or indeed to go deeply into questions of "style," but we may be tempted to explore farther, and if we examine such cafés as, for instance, those at El Biar or Birkadem, we shall find the walls ornamented with arabesques, sometimes half concealed under whitewash, and the arcades and conical-domed roofs and doorways covered with curious patterns.

In this way we pass the day, often lingering about one spot in most vagrant fashion, till nightfall, when the last diligence comes crashing in, and stops to change its wretched horses. We take our places quickly in the *interieur*, and are wedged in between little soft white figures with black eyes and stained finger-nails, who stare at us with a fixed and stony stare, all the way back to Algiers. Another day we spend in the *Jardin d'Essai*, the garden of acclimatization, where we may wander in December amidst groves of summer flowers, and where every variety of tree and shrub is brought together for study and comparison. Through the kindness of the director, we are enabled to make studies of some rare and curious tropical plants ; but there is a little too much formality and an artificial atmosphere about the place, that spoils it for sketching, although nothing can control, or render formal, the wild strength of the gigantic aloes, or make the palmtrees grow in line.

From the " Garden of Marengo," just outside the western gates, we obtain the sketch given on the opposite page ; and from the heights behind the Casbah, some beautiful distant views across the plain of the Mitidja. Of one of these an artistic traveller writes : " Standing on a ridge of the Sahel, far beneath lies the Bay of Algiers, from this particular point thrown into a curve

OVER THE SEA.

so exquisite and subtle as to be wellnigh inimitable by art, the value of the curve being enhanced by the long level line of the Mitidja plain immediately behind, furnishing the horizontal line of repose so indispensable to calm beauty of landscape ; whilst in the background the faintly indicated serrated summits of the Atlas chain preserve the whole picture from monotony. The curve of shore, the horizontal bar of plain, the scarcely more than suggested angles of the mountains, form a combination of contrasting yet harmonizing lines of infinite loveliness, which Nature would ever paint anew for us in the fresh tints of the morning, with a brush dipped in golden sunshine and soft filmy mist, and with a broad sweep of cool blue shadow over the foreground."

But our favorite rendezvous, our principal " Champ de Mars," was a little Arab cemetery, about six miles from Algiers, on the heights westward, in the direction of Sidi Ferruch, and near to a little Arab village called the " Bouzareah." This spot combined a wondrous view both of sea and land, with a foreground of beauty not easy to depict. It was a half-deserted cemetery, with tombs of Marabout priests over which the palm-trees waved, and little gravestones here and there surmounted with crescents. Sheltered from the sun's rays, hidden from the sight of passers-by, surrounded with a profusion of aloes, palms, cacti, and an infinite variety of shrubs and flowers peeping out between the palmettos, that spread their leaves like fans upon the ground, — it combined everything that could be desired.

Here we worked, sitting close to one of the tombs for its shade, with the hush of the breeze, the distant sighing sound of the sea, the voices of bees and butterflies, the flutter of leaves, and one other sound that intermingled with strange

monotony of effect close to our ears, which puzzled
us sorely to account for at first. It turned out
to be a snore ; the custodian of one of the tombs
was sleeping inside with his fathers, little dreaming of our proximity. We struck up an acquaintance with him, after a few days of coyness on his
part, and finally made him a friend. For a few
sous a day he acted as outpost for us, to keep
off Arab boys and any other intruders, and before we left was induced to sit and be included
in a sketch. He winced a little at this, and
we confess to an inward reproach for having
thus degraded him. He did not like it, but he
sat it out and had his portrait taken like any
Christian dog ; he took money for his sin, and
finally (by way of expiation, let us hope) drank
up our dirty palette-water at the end of the
day !

If there is one spot in all Algeria most dear
to a Mussulman's heart, most sacred to a Mara-

bout's memory, it must surely be this peaceful garden of aloes and palms, where flowers ever grow, where the sun shines from the moment of its rising until it sinks beneath the western sea; where, if anywhere on this earth, the faithful will be the first to know of the Prophet's coming, and where they will always be ready to meet him. But if it be dear to a Mussulman's heart, it is also dear to a Christian's, for it has taught us more in a few weeks than we can unlearn in years. We cannot sit here day by day without learning several truths, more forcibly than by any teaching of our schools; taking in, as it were, the mysteries of light and shade, and the various phases of the atmosphere, — taking them all to heart, so that they influence our work for years to come.

How often have we, at the Uffizi or at the Louvre, envied the power and skill of a master, whose work we have vainly endeavored to imitate ; and what would we not have given in those days, to achieve something that seemed to approach, ever so little, to the power and beauty of color of a Titian or a Paul Veronese.*

Is it mere heresy in art, or is it a brighter light dawning upon us here, that seems to say that we have learned and achieved more, in studying the glowing limbs of an Arab child as it plays amongst these wild palmettos, because we worked with a background of real sea and sky, and because in the painting of the child we had not to learn any "master's" trick of color, nor to follow conventional lines?

And do we not, amongst other things, learn to distinguish between the true and conventional rendering of the form, color, and character of palm-trees, aloes, and cacti?

---

* And have we not, generally, imbibed more of the trick or method of color, of the master, than of his inspiration, — more, in short, of the real than the ideal?

First, of the palm. Do we not soon discover
how much more of beauty, of suggested strength,
of grace, lightness,
and variety of color
and texture, there
is in this one stem
that we vainly try
to depict in a wood
engraving, than we
had previously any
conception of? And
how opposed to facts
are the conventional
methods of drawing
palm - trees (often
with a straight stem
and uniform leaves looking like a feather broom
on a straight stick), which we may find in almost
any illustrated book representing Eastern scenes,
from Constantinople to the Sea of Galilee !

Take, for instance, as a proof of variety in color and grandeur of aspect, the group of palm-trees at the Bouzareah (one of which we have sketched), that have stood guard over the Mohammedan tombs for perhaps a hundred years; stained with time, and shattered with their fierce battle with the storms that sweep over the promontory with terrible force. Look at the beauty of their lines, at the glorious color of their young leaves, and the deep orange of those they have shed, like the plumage of some gigantic bird; one of their number has fallen from age, and lies crossways on the ground, half concealed in the long grass and shrubs, and it has lain there, to our knowledge, undisturbed for years. To paint the sun setting on these glowing stems, and to catch the shadows of their sharp pointed leaves, as they are traced at one period of the day on the white walls of the tombs, is worth long waiting to be able to note down; and to hit the right tint, to depict such shadows truly, is an exciting triumph to us.

Second, of the aloe; and here we make as great a discovery as with the palm. Have we not been taught (in paintings) from our youth up, that the aloe puts forth its blue riband-like leaves in uniform fashion, like so many starched pennants, which painters often express with one or two strokes of the brush; and are we not told by botanists that it flowers but once in a hundred years?

Look at that aloe hedge-row a little distance from us, that stretches across the country like a long blue rippling wave on a calm sea, and which, as we approach it, seems thrown up fantastically and irregularly by breakers to a height of six or eight feet, and which (like the sea), on a nearer view, changes its opaque cold blue tint to a rich transparent green and gold. Approach them closely, walk under their colossal leaves, avoid their sharp spear-points, and touch their soft pulpy stems. What wonderful variety there is in their forms, what transparent beauty of color; what eccentric shadows they cast upon each other, and with what a grand spiral sweep some of the young shoots rear upwards! So tender and pliable are they, that in some positions a child might snap their leaves, and yet so wonderful is the distribution of strength, that they would resist at spear-point the approach of a lion, and almost turn a charge of cavalry. If we snap off the point of one of the leaves it is a needle, and a thread clings to it which we may peel off down the stem a yard long, — needle and thread, — nature-pointed, nature-threaded! Should not artists see these things? Should not poets dream of them?

Here we are inclined to ask, if the aloe flowers but once in a hundred years, how is it that everywhere in Algeria we see plants of all ages with their long flowering stems, some ten or twelve feet high? Have they combined this year to flower, or are botanists at fault?

Of the cactus, which also grows in wild profusion, we could say almost as much as of the palms and aloes, but it might seem like repetition. Suffice it, that our studies of their separate leaves were the minutest and most rewarding labor we achieved, and that, until we had painted the cactus and the palmetto growing together, we had never understood the meaning of " tropical vegetation."

Many other subjects we obtain at the Bouzareah ; simple perhaps, and apparently not worth recording, but of immense value to a student of nature. Is it nothing, for instance, for a painter to have springing up before him, in this clear atmosphere, delicate stems of grass, six feet high, falling over in spray of golden leaves against a background of blue sea ; darting upward, sheer, bright, and transparent from a bank covered with the prickly pear, that looks, by contrast, like the rock-work from which a fountain springs? Is it nothing to see amongst all this wondrous overgrowth of gigantic leaves, and amongst the tender creepers and the flowers, the curious knotted and twisted stem of the vine, trailing serpent-like on the ground, its surface worn smooth with time?

It is well worth coming to North Africa in winter, if only to see the flowers; but of these we cannot trust ourselves to speak, — they must be seen and painted.

It is difficult to tear ourselves away from this spot, and especially tempting to dwell upon these details, because they have seldom been treated of before; but perhaps the question may occur to some, Are such subjects as we have depicted worth painting, or, indeed, of any prolonged or separate study? Let us endeavor to answer it by another question. Are the waves worth painting, by themselves? Has it not occurred to one or two artists (not to many, we admit) that the waves of the sea have never yet been adequately painted, and have never had their due, so to speak, because it has always been considered necessary to introduce something else into the composition, be it only a rope, a spar, or a deserted ship? Has it not been discovered (though only of late years) that there is scope for imagination and poetry, and all the elements of a great and enthralling picture, in the drawing of waves alone; and should there not be, if nobly treated, interest enough in a group of colossal vegetation in a brilliant atmosphere, without the usual conventional adjuncts of figures and buildings?

So far, whilst sketching at the Bouzareah, we have spoken only of the foreground; but we have been all the time in the presence of the most wonderful panorama of sea and land, and have watched so many changing aspects from these heights, that we might fill a chapter in describing them alone. The view northward over the Mediterranean, westward towards Sidi Ferruch, southward across the plains to the Atlas, eastward towards Algiers and the mountains of Kabylia beyond ; each point so distant from the other that, according to the wind or time of day, it partook of quite distinct aspects, fill up so many pictures in our mind's eye that a book might be written, called " The Bouzareah," as seen under the different phases of sunshine and storm.

It has often been objected to these Eastern scenes, that they have " no atmosphere," and no gradation of middle distance ; that there is not enough repose about them, that they lack mystery and are altogether wanting in the poetry of cloudland. But there are clouds. We have seen, for the last few mornings (looking through the arched windows of the great aloe-leaves), little companies of small white clouds, casting clearly defined shadows across the distant sea, and breaking up the horizon line with their soft white folds

" They come like shadows, so depart,"

reappearing and disappearing by some mysterious law, but seldom culminating in rain.

Yes, there are clouds. Look this time far
away towards the horizon line across the bay, and
watch that rolling sea which looks like foam, that
rises higher and higher as we watch it, darkening
the sky, and soon enveloping us in a kind of sea-
fog, through which the sun gleams dimly red,
whilst the white walls of the tombs appear cold
and gray against a leaden sky. See it all pass
away again across the plain of the Mitidja, and
disappear in the shadows of the lesser Atlas.
There is a hush in the breeze and all is bright
again, but a storm is coming.

Take shelter, if you have courage, *inside* one
of the Marabouts' tombs (there is plenty of space),
whilst a tempest rages that should wake the dead
before Mahomet's coming. Sit and wait in there,
perhaps an hour, whilst one or two strong gusts of
wind pass over, and then all is still again; and
so dark that we can see nothing inside but the
light of a pipe in one corner. We get impatient,

thinking that it is passing off. But it comes at last. It breaks over the tombs, and tears through the plantation, with a tremendous surging sound, putting to flight the Arabs on guard, who wrap their bournouses about them and hurry off to the village, with the cry of " Allah il Allah "; leaving the care of the tombs to the palms, that have stood guard over them so long. O, how they fight and struggle in the wind! how they creak, and moan, and strike against one another, like human creatures in the thick of battle! How they rally side by side, and wrestle with the wind, — crashing down suddenly against the walls of the tomb, and scattering their leaves over us; then rallying again, and fighting the storm with human energy and persistence!

It is a fearful sight, — the rain falling in masses, but nearly horizontally, and with such density that we can see but a few yards from our place of shelter; and it is a fearful sound, to hear the palm-trees shriek in the wind.

There was one part of the scene we could not
describe, one which no other than Dante's pen
or Doré's pencil could give any idea of; we could
not depict the confused muttering sound and
grinding clatter (if we may call it so) that the
battered and wounded aloes made amongst themselves, like maimed and dying combatants trodden
under foot.   Many scenes in nature have been
compared to a battle-field; we have seen sheaves
of corn blown about by the wind, looking like the
tents of a routed host; but this scene was beyond
parallel, — the hideous contortion, the melancholy
aspect of destruction, the disfigured limbs in
hopeless wreck, the weird and ghastly forms that
writhed and groaned aloud, as the storm made
havoc with them.

And they made havoc with each other.   What
would the reader say, if he saw the wounds in-
flicted by some of the young leaves on the parent
stems, — how they pierce and transfix, and some-

times *saw* into each other, with their sharp serrated edges, as they sway backwards and forwards in the wind. He would say perhaps that no seamonster or devil-fish could seem more horrible, and we could wish him no wilder vision than to be near them at night, when disturbed by the wind.

We have scarcely alluded to the palmetto leaves and branches that filled the air, to the sound of rushing water, to the distant roar of the sea, nor to many other aspects of the storm. It lasted not much more than an hour, but the water covered the floor of our little temple before the rain subsided, and the ground a few feet off where we had sat was completely under water. Everything was steaming with vapor, but the land was refreshed, and the dark earth was richer than we had seen it for months, — there would be no dust in Algiers until to-morrow.

ARABS.

CHAPTER VII.

BLIDAH. — MEDEAH. — THE ATLAS MOUNTAINS.

THE Atlas Mountains, of which we have spoken so often, are almost separated from the hills of the Sahel on which the town of Algiers is built, by the broad plain of the Mitidja, averaging between twenty and thirty miles across; and at the inland extremity of this plain, nestling close under the shadow of the lesser Atlas, is situated the town of Blidah, half Arab, half French, with its little population of European colonists and traders, — principally orange-merchants, who here pass their monotonous, semi-successful lives, varied by occasional earthquakes and Arab *émeutes*.

It was not particularly to see Blidah, but because it was on the high-road to the Atlas Mountains, and to Medeah, a strongly fortified town situated 2,900 feet above the sea-level, — approached by a military road cut through the celebrated gorge of "La Chiffa," — that two of our party left Algiers on horseback, on the 14th of December, on a sketching expedition.

We made many other interesting tours ; but it will be sufficient for our purpose to speak of two expeditions, — the one to Medeah, the other to the celebrated "Fort Napoléon," on the Kabyle Hills.

It seems to say something for the peculiarly invigorating character of the climate, that, at an average temperature of 70° Fahrenheit, our little horses did their thirty or forty miles a day, laden with our well-stored saddle-bags and sketching paraphernalia ; and it speaks volumes for the security with which travellers can move about from town to town, that we were merely by

chance provided with firearms, and travelled without guide or escort.*

We pass through the eastern gate of Algiers
before sunrise, and winding up the hills behind
Mustapha Supérieure (keeping to the road), begin
to descend on the southern side, and have the
broad plain of the Mitidja before us, just as the
day is breaking. As we come down towards the
plain we pass several farms of the French colonists, and here and there a tobacco plantation
where both Arabs and French are employed. At
Birkadem, which is in the midst of a farming
district, we halt to breakfast, and run considerable risk of getting into a controversy on French
colonization with some friendly and pleasant but
rather desponding agriculturists. But, happily for
ourselves and for our readers, we do not attempt
to master the subject, and with a sketch of the

* At the time we speak of journeys into the interior were
much less frequent than they are now, when there is a railway to Blidah and a diligence to the Fort Napoléon.

little Moorish café with its marble columns and arcades, we continue our journey; over a wide waste, — half moorland, half desert, — passing at intervals little oases of cultivation, with houses, shrubs, and gardens surrounding. Straight before us, apparently only a few miles off, but in reality twenty, stretches the chain of the lesser Atlas, the dark shadows here and there pointing out the approaches to a higher range beyond.

At the foot of the mountains we can distinctly see with our glasses the white Moorish houses and villas that are built near Blidah, and the thick clusters of trees that shelter them. Our way across the plain for the next two or three hours is rather solitary, and although we keep up a steady pace, we seem to get no nearer to our destination. We pass a number of Arabs leading camels, and overtake a troop of twenty or thirty donkeys, laden with goods and ridden by their owners (who sit upon the top of their piles), shambling along almost as fast as a horse can trot. They beat us hollow before noon, because they never stop, and reach Bouffarik, the midday resting-place, long before us.

At Bouffarik we are again amongst the colonists, and hear the peculiar French dialect of Provence and Languedoc, with occasional snatches of German and Maltese. We rest until about two hours of sunset, and become thoroughly imbued with the idea that we must be again in the south of France ; so completely have the French realized, in the midst of an African plain, the dull uniformity of a poor French town, with its "place," its one street of cobble-stones, and its two rows of trees. Here we can obtain bad coffee, just as we can in France, and read the *Moniteur*, but four days old. It is altogether French, and when the white Arab mare belonging to one of our party turns restive at starting again, and proceeds through the village on its hind legs, it is just in time to remind us that it was here that Horace Vernet worked, and painted those rampant white steeds that we know so well in the centre of his battle pictures.   The war-horse (with the light upon him) was more to Horace Vernet, perhaps, than the glory of the whole plain of the Mitidja; but how he could have lived in Algeria so long, and have been so little influenced by the scene around him, it is hard to tell.

It is tempting (indeed it is almost impossible to avoid) at Bouffarik, going a little into the question of colonization, and speaking from personal observation of the progress made during the last few years.   But as English people care little or nothing for the prospects of Algeria, we will merely remark, *en passant*, that the insurmountable evil of Algeria being too near the home country seems to blight its prospects even here, and that the want of confidence displayed by private capitalists retards all progress.   Nearly all the capital em-

ployed by the colonists at Bouffarik and Blidah
has been raised by a paternal government; but,
notwithstanding help from the home country, the
tide of wealth neither flows nor ebbs with great
rapidity.

At Bouffarik we see the Arabs calmly settled
under French rule, and learning the arts of peace;
taking to husbandry and steam ploughs, and otherwise progressing in a scientific and peaceful direction. We see them in the evening, sitting by
their cottages with their half-naked children, looking prosperous and happy enough, and hear them
droning to them in that monotonous "sing-song"
that is so irritating to the ear. There is a musician
at the door of our hostelry now, who is as great
a nuisance as any Italian organ-grinder in May-
fair; he taps on a little piece of stretched parch-
ment, and howls without ceasing. It is given to
the inhabitants of some countries, who have what
is commonly called "no ear for music," to hum

and to drone in more sensitive ears to the point
of distraction, and it seems to be the special attri-
bute of the Arab to fill the air with monotonous
sounds; when he is on a journey or resting from
it, it is the same, — he hums and moans like a
creature in torment. In contact with Europeans
we perhaps see him at his worst; for, however
orderly and useful a member of society he may
be, however neat and clean, there is something
cringing and artificial in him at the best. But
we must hasten on to Blidah.

Again we cross a wide plain, again do we overtake and are overtaken by the tribe of donkeys;
and just as the sun goes down we enter the city
gates together, dismounting in the principal square,
which is filled with idlers, chiefly French soldiers
and poor Arabs who have learned to beg. We
had chosen the time for this journey when the
moon was nearly full, and our first near view of
the town was by moonlight. Nothing can be

conceived more beautiful than Blidah by night, with its little white domes and towers, and the mountains looming indistinctly in the background. In the Moorish quarter the tower of the principal Mosque stands out clearly defined in the moon-light, whilst all around it cluster the little flat-roofed houses, set in masses of dark foliage, — the olives and the date-trees, and the sharp-pointed spires of the cypresses just tinged with a silver light. So peaceful, so beautiful does it look at night, so complete the repose with which we have always associated Blidah, that it is a rude disen-chantment to learn that but a few years ago this city was upheaved and tossed about like the waves of the sea. In 1825 eight or nine thou-sand people perished from an earthquake ; and in 1866 a lady who was staying at the hotel thus wrote home to her friends : —

" I was roused from sleep by a sound as of some one beating the floor above and the walls on every side.

It increased rapidly in violence, till the whole house shook and rocked and seemed giving way beneath our feet. I saw the wall in the corner of the room split open, and immediately afterwards masses of plaster fell from the ceiling and walls, bringing clouds of dust and a darkness as of night.

.   .   .   .   .

"On the *Place* it was a fearful scene: people came tearing down the neighboring streets, women and children ran aimlessly hither and thither, shrieking wildly, men uttering hoarse sounds of terror, whilst the ground heaved and trembled beneath our feet, and we gazed at the surrounding houses in expectant horror; it seemed as if they must fall like a pack of cards. The young trees rocked and swayed, the flagstaff waved backwards and forwards, — the wind moaning, the rain pouring down, whilst above all rose, ever and anon, the sound of cavalry trumpets and the rolling of the drum, calling on the troops to quit their tottering barracks. The Arabs alone stalked about unmoved, shrugging their shoulders and muttering, 'It is destiny!'"

The air is delightful at Blidah, and the little country houses, with their groves of orange-trees,

their gardens and vineyards, have been pointed
out by travellers as some of the most desirable
spots on earth. The extract above may tend to
qualify the longings of some people ; but we
should be inclined to take our chance at Blidah,
as the Neapolitans do near Vesuvius, — there are
so many compensations.

Early in the morning we are again on our way,
and as we leave the western gate, the donkeys,
with their dirty drivers, scramble out with us and
again play the game of the tortoise and the hare.
The gorge of La Chiffa is one of the principal approaches to the mountains, through which a military road is cut to Medeah. The first part is
wild and rocky, the road passing between almost
perpendicular cliffs, carried sometimes by masonry
over a chasm at a height of several hundred feet.
We ride for miles through a valley of almost
solitary grandeur, with no sounds but the rushing of the torrent and the occasional cries of mon-

keys. We pass by one celebrated waterfall called the "Ruisseau des Singes," and are otherwise reminded of the presence of monkeys by their pelting us with large stones, which they dislodge from their hiding-places above our heads.

We are at times so shut in by the rocks that we can scarcely discover any outlet; but after a few hours' ascent we come suddenly upon quite a different scene. What is it that delights the eye and that thrills us with pleasurable emotions, calling up memories of green lanes and England, pastoral? 'T is the plash of water, and the trickling, tinkling play of a running stream, winding and winding down to the swollen torrent that we crossed just now. Here under the shadow and shelter of the mountains — refreshed by rains that they in the plains know not of, and where the heat of a midday sun can scarcely approach — we find a cottage, a little farm, green pastures, cattle grazing, trees, flowers, and children; the stream flowing through all, bright, deep, and sparkling, with green banks, bulrushes and lilies of the valley of the Atlas. A few poor emigrants have settled down in this corner of the world as quietly, and we may add as securely, as if a sandy plain did not divide them from everything kindred and civilized.

We make our midday halt under the shade of chestnut-trees, and sketch; one great defect of our drawings being that they are far too pastoral, — they would not be admitted by judges to represent Africa at all! Nothing in this land of strong contrasts could equal the change from Nature, untilled, unfruitful, stern, and forbidding, to this little farm-house, as it might be in Wales, surrounded by trees and watered by a sparkling stream.

Continuing our journey up the gorge, walking, riding, clambering, and resting by turns, we do not reach Medeah until after dark. During the

last few miles our horses are troublesome, and
will not be persuaded to pass close to any rock
or brushwood, being evidently nervous of some
sudden attack or surprise ; and so we creep along
silently and in single file, trusting chiefly to our
horses to keep to the path.   At last the long-
looked-for lights of Medeah appear, and in a
quarter of an hour afterwards we are inside the
fortifications ; and with a " *Voyageurs, monsieur* "
to the sentinel at the gate, we pass under the dark
arches of a Roman aqueduct, — casting a deep
shadow over the town as the moon shines out,
now obscured again by a passing cloud, like some
solemn dissolving view of Roman power, or phan-
tom monument of the past.

At Medeah we find everything much the same
as at Blidah ; a little rougher and poorer perhaps,
but the same mixture of French and Moorish
buildings.   Fine old mosques, courtyards after the
style of the Alhambra, and carved doorways of

very early date; but brick fortifications, young French soldiers, *estaminéts,* and a " Place " with half-dead trees, are more prominent features; and here, at a height of nearly 3,000 feet above the sea, set deep in the heart of the Atlas, civilization may again be seen doing its work, — the Arabs indulging in absinthe freely, and playing at cards with their conquerors.

The beautiful mountain scenery south of Medeah led us to spend some time in sketching and in exploring the country. In spite of its wildness and solitariness we could wander about with perfect security, within a day or two's journey of the French outposts. The crisp keen air at this altitude tempted us on and on, through the most deserted region that can be imagined. The mountain-ranges to the south were like an undulating sea, divided from us by lesser hills and little plains, with here and there valleys, green and cultivated; but the prevailing character of the scenery was rocky and barren. The great beauty was in the clouds that passed over at intervals, spreading a grateful shade, and casting wonderful shadows on the rocks. The rain would fall heavily through them sometimes for three or four minutes, like summer showers, and the little dried-up torrent beds would trickle for a while; the Arabs would collect a few drops, and then all would be gone, — the clouds, the rivulets, and every sign of moisture on the ground, — and the mountains would stand out sharp and clear against the sky, with that curious pinky hue so often seen in the background of pictures of Eastern scenes.

. Here we could pitch our tent in the deepest solitude, and romance as much as we pleased without fear of interruption. The only variation to the almost death-like silence that prevailed would be the distant cry of a jackall, which disturbed us for a moment, or the moaning of the wind in some far-off valley, for the air seemed never still on these heights. A stray monkey or two would come and furtively peep at our proceedings, but would be off again in an instant, and there were no birds; indeed, since we left Blidah we had scarcely heard their voices. The few Arab tribes that cultivated the valleys seldom came near us; so that we sometimes heard no voices but our own from morning till night.

One day proved an exception. We had been making a drawing of the prospect due south, in order to get the effect of the sun's rays upon a sandy plateau that stretched between us and the next range of mountains : it was little more than a study of color and effect, for there was not much to break the monotony of the subject, — a sand-plain bounded by barren rocks. We had nearly finished our work, when two dark specks appeared suddenly on the sky-line, and quickly descending the rocks, began to cross the plain towards us. With our telescope we soon made out that they

were horsemen at full gallop, and we could tell
this, not by the figures themselves, but by the
long shadows that the afternoon sun cast from
them upon the plain.   In a few minutes they
rode up to our tent.   They were not, as our
porters had insisted, some Arabs on a reconnoi-
tring expedition, but two American gentlemen on
hired horses from Algiers, who were scampering
about the country without any guide or escort.
They had come from Milianah that day, they
would be at Blidah to-morrow, and at Algiers
the next day, in time to "catch the boat for
Europe!"

There was an end to all romance about desert
scenes and being "alone with Nature"; we could
not get rid of the Western world; we were tourists,
and nothing more.   But it was pleasant to hear
the English language spoken, and delightful to
record that these gentlemen neither bragged of
their exploits nor favored us with what are called

in Europe "Americanisms." In short, we are able
to speak of our interview (they came back with us
as far as Medeah) without repeating any of those
bits of smart conversation that seem inseparable
from the record of such rencontres. These gentlemen had taken a glance at a great deal in four or
five days, and had been (perhaps it did not much
matter) once or twice into a little danger; they
had seen the cedar forests, the "Fort Napoléon,"
and the principal sights, and were now on their
way home. They had, however, done one thing
in which they evidently felt unmixed satisfaction,
though they did not express it in so many words,
— they had been rather *farther* into the interior
than any of their countrymen.

Before leaving the mountains we should answer
a question that we have been asked repeatedly,
"What of the African lion, so celebrated by Jules
Gérard?" We answer, that we did not penetrate
far enough for "sport" of this kind; indeed, we

K

scarcely ever heard of any lions. Once only our horses stopped and trembled violently, and would not pass a thicket without a long détour; and once (only once) we heard the lion's roar, not far off. It is a sound that carries a dread with it not soon forgotten, and the solemnity of which, when echoed from the mountains, it is not easy to describe. Perhaps the only person who was ever flippant in speaking of lions was Gordon Cumming; but then he used to go amongst them (according to his own account) single-handed, to "select specimens" before firing!

In the solitude of these mountain wanderings we had opportunities of seeing one phase of Arab life that we had really come out to see, and which was alone worth the journey. We had started early one morning from Blidah, but not so early that, in deference to the wishes of some of our companions, we had first attended service in a chapel dedicated to "Our Lady of Succor." We

went into the little building, which, like some
rare exotic, was flourishing alone, surrounded by
the most discordant elements, — situated hard by
a mosque and close to some noisy Arab dwellings.
Service was being performed in the usual manner,
the priests were bowing before a tinsel cross, and
praying, in a language of their own, to a colored
print of "Our Lady" in a gilt frame. There
were the customary chantings, the swinging of
censers, the creaking of chairs, the interchanging
of glances, and the paying of sous. Sins were
confessed through a hole in the wall, and holy
water was administered to the faithful with a
brush. Everything was conducted with perfect
decorum, and was (as it seemed to an eyewit-
ness) the most materialistic expression of devotion
it were possible to devise.

Before the evening of the same day we make
a halt amongst the mountains. A few yards
from us we see in the evening light a promon-

tory ; upon it some figures, motionless, and nearly the same color as the rocks, — Arabs watching the setting sun. The twilight has faded so rapidly into darkness, that we have soon to put by our work, and can see no objects distinctly, excepting this promontory ; on which the sun still shines through some unseen valley, and lights up the figures as they kneel in prayer. The solemnity of the scene could hardly be conveyed to the mind of the reader in words, its picturesqueness we should altogether fail to do justice to ; but its beauty and suggestiveness set us upon a train of thought which, in connection with the ceremony of the morning, we may be pardoned for dwelling upon in a few words.

It was not the first nor the last time that we had witnessed the Arabs at prayer, and had studied with a painter's eye their attitudes of devotion, the religious fervor in their faces, and their perfect *abandon.* The charm of the scene was in its primitive aspect, and in the absence of all the accessories which Europeans are taught from their youth up to connect in some way with every act of public worship. And who could help being struck by the sight of all this earnestness, — at these heartfelt prayers? What does the Arab see in this mystery of beauty, in its daily recurring splendor and decline? Shall we say that the rising and the setting of the sun behind the hills may not (to the rude souls of men who have learned their all from Nature) point out the entrance of that Paradise which their simple faith has taught them they shall one day enter and possess?

If it were possible in these days, when religious art assumes the most fantastic forms, to create ever so slight a reaction against a school which has perhaps held its own too long, — if it were not heresy to set forth as the noblest aim for a painter, that he should depict the deepest emo-

tion, the simplest faith, the most heartfelt devotion, without the accessories of purple and fine
linen, without marble columns or gilded shrines,
without furniture, without Madonnas, and without
paste, — then we might point confidently to the
picture before us to aid our words. What if the
heaven prayed for and the prophet worshipped
seem to a Christian unorthodox and worse, —
there is sincerity here, there is faith, devotion,
ecstasy, adoration. What more, indeed, does the
painter hope for; what does he seek ; and what
more has he ever found in the noblest work of
Christian art ?

If he lack enthusiasm, still, before a scene so
strange, let him think for a moment what manner
of worship this of the Arabs is, and contrast their
system with that of the Vatican. The religion of
the Arabs is a very striking thing, and its position
and influence on their lives might put many
professing Christians to the blush. An honest,

earnest faith is theirs, be it right or wrong. If
we examine it at all, we find it something more
than a silly superstition; we find that it has been
"a firm belief and hope amongst twelve millions
of men in Arabia alone, holding its place in their
hearts for more than twelve hundred years." It
is a religion of Duty, an acting up to certain fixed
principles and defined laws of life, untrammelled
by many ceremonies, unshaken by doubts; a following out to the letter the written law, as laid
down for them by Mahomet, as the rule and principle of their lives. If the whole system of the
Mohammedan faith breaks down (as we admit it
does) on examination, it does not affect our position, namely, that we have here an exhibition of
religious fervor which seldom reaches to fanaticism,
and is essentially sincere. Regarding the scene
from a purely artistic point of view, we can imagine no more fitting subject for a painter than
this group of Arabs at their devotions, — Nature

their temple, its altar the setting sun, their faces towards Mecca, their hearts towards the Prophet, their every attitude breathing devotion and faith.

Setting aside all questions of orthodoxy, regarding for our particular purpose both civilized and uncivilized worshippers under their general religious aspect, — how would it "strike that stranger" who, descending from another planet, wondered why, if men's Duty was so clearly placed before them, they did not follow it, — how would he view the two great phases of religious worship? Whose religion would seem most inspiring, whose temple most fitting, whose altar most glorious, whose religion the most free from question, — the modern and enlightened, intrenched in orthodoxy and enthroned in state; or the benighted and unregenerate, but earnest, nature-loving, and always sincere?

We shall have perhaps (if we make a serious study of these subjects and put our heart into the work) to unlearn something that we have been taught about the steady painting of Madonnas and angels in our schools; but, if we do no more than make one or two sketches of such scenes as the above, we shall have added to our store of knowledge in a rough and ready way, and have familiarized ourselves with the sight of what — though barbaric — is noble and true.

KABYLES.

CHAPTER VIII.

KABYLIA. — THE FORT NAPOLÉON.

IT was almost impossible to take up a news-paper in Algiers, or to converse for five minutes in a café or at the club, without the "question Kabyle" cropping up in some paragraph or conversation. Every day there came contradictory news about the war, that it would really be over to-morrow, or the next day, or the next week. It had lasted with more or less activity for thirty years, but now at last the smouldering embers seemed to be dying out.

The Djurjura Mountains stretching eastward into Kabylia, which we knew so well in their peaceful aspect, with the sun shining upon their snow-clad summits from morning till night, were still the theatre of war. In the heart of the mountains, about sixty miles from Algiers, and at a height of 3,000 feet above the sea, the French army was busily engaged in building a fortress, in order to keep the Kabyles at bay and give protection to the colonists ; and whilst this work was progressing with wonderful rapidity, the outposts of the army were carrying on a guerilla warfare with the unsubdued tribes. Their camps were pitched on the various heights, and the sound of the morning *réveille* was generally succeeded by the "ping" of the rifle from some concealed Kabyles, and by a quick return volley from the French outposts.

We went to the Fort Napoléon at the invitation of some French officers, who, when they wrote to us, imagined (as all French people had imagined a hundred times before) that the war was over, and that it would be a good opportunity to visit the camp and the fort, in process of construction.* Two easy days' journey on horseback, halting for the night at a caravanserai called Les Issers, brought us to Tiziouzou, a small town and military depôt on the borders of Kabylia, at the foot of the mountains, and but a few miles from the fort. At Les Issers we slept upon the ground, each man by the side of his own horse, as there was neither stabling nor sleeping accommodation to be had in the inn, which was crowded, before we arrived, with troops and war *matériel*. To reach this, our first night's halting-place, we had had some rough riding, ending by fording in the evening a rapid river which rose above the saddle-girths and nearly upset our active little horses. The night was starlight, and we lay down

---

* General Randon laid the first stone of the Fort Napoléon in June, 1857. This fort, which occupies an area of more than twenty acres, and is built on most irregular ground, was built in a few months.

about fifty together, with fires burning in a circle round us, to prevent any surprise.

The route from Les Issers to Tiziouzou was crowded with baggage-wagons sticking in the mud, and with immense droves of camels and donkeys on their way to the fort. The late rains had almost obliterated the military road (which was said to extend all the way from Algiers to the Fort Napoléon), and in some places it was turned into a river. The greater part of our route had been wild and uncultivated, but as we came near to Tiziouzou and approached the mountains, every valley was luxuriant with vegetation, fig-trees and olives grew in abundance, the former of enormous size. But nearly every inhabitant was French, and we, who had come to sketch and to see the Kabyles, were as yet disappointed at finding none but French soldiers, European camp-followers, and camel-drivers on the way; and when we arrived at Tiziouzou, we were so shut in by mountains on all sides, that even the heights of Beni-Raten were concealed from view. It was fortunate that we obtained the shelter of a little inn on the night of our arrival, for the rain fell steadily in sheets of water, until our wooden house was soaked through, and stood like an island in the midst of a lake.

We sent our horses back to Algiers, and carrying our own knapsacks, set off in the early morning to walk up to the fort. A lively cantinière, attached to a regiment of Zouaves camped near Tiziouzou, walked with us and led the way, past one or two half-deserted Kabyle villages, by a short cut to the camp. The military road by which the artillery had been brought up was about fifteen miles, but by taking the steeper paths we must have reduced the distance by more than half. At one point of the way the bare mountain-side was so steep and slippery with the late rain, that it was almost impossible to ascend it; but some

Arabs, with an eye to business worthy of the Western world, had stationed themselves here with their camels to drag up pedestrians; a camel's tail was let for two sous, and was in great request. The latter part of the ascent was through forests, and groves of olive and cork trees, looking cool and gray amongst the mass of rich vegetation, through which we had sometimes to cut a path. It was a wild walk, but our merry little cantinière was so active and entertaining that we, encumbered with knapsacks, had enough to do to keep up with her, and indeed to comprehend the rapid little French histories that she favored us with. Every now and then we heard through the trees the strains of "Partant pour la Syrie," or the rattle of a regimental drum, and came suddenly upon working parties on the road, which the army boasts was made practicable in three months. After about four hours' clambering we again emerge upon the road, near the summit, and in a few minutes more come in sight of the fort and the pretty white tents of the camps on the surrounding hills.

Here we must pause a few minutes, to give a short account of the last great expedition against the Kabyles in this district in 1857, as related by Lieutenant-Colonel Walmisley : —

" Daylight dawned upon the Kabyle hills on the morning of the 24th June, and its light streamed over the serried ranks of the second division, as, under the command of General Mac-Mahon, the head of the column marched out of the lines of Aboudid. Before it lay the heights of Icheriden, with its village and triple row of barricades, behind which the men of the Beni Menguillet anxiously watched the progress of the foe. The path of the column lay along a moun-tain ridge, and it was strange to see that column of between six and seven thousand men advan-cing quietly and composedly, the birds singing

8 *   L

around them, the Kabyles crowning every available hillock, the hawks and eagles slowly wheeling in large circles over their heads, and the bright rays of the morning sun gleaming on brighter bayonets.

. . . . .

" The Kabyle barricades remained black and silent as ever ; not a bournous was to be seen, as the 54th and the Zouaves received orders to carry the position at the point of the bayonet. Before them lay a ridge covered with brushwood, affording capital shelter ; but at about sixty or seventy paces from the stockades the brush had been cleared away, and now the occasional gleam of a bayonet, the report of a musket or two fired against the stockade, the loud ringing of the trumpets, as they gave forth in inspiriting tones the *pas de charge,* and the wild shouting of the men, as they pushed their way forward, told of the progress of the attack.

"Still the same stern, heavy silence reigned over the hostile village. Was it indeed deserted, or was it the silence of despair? But now the bugle-notes became shriller and more exciting, the shots quicker and more steady, as, emerging from the bush, the attacking column rushed forward to the attack. Sixty paces of greensward were before them; but instantly, and as if by magic, a thousand reports broke the silence of the dark stockades, a wild yell rose from their defenders as the hail of lead fell on the advancing regiments, and a long line of dead marked the advance. The Kabyles leaning their pieces over the joints of the trees, where they were fitted into each other, and through crevices and loop-holes, offered little or no mark themselves to the shot; whilst not a ball of theirs missed its aim.

"But the Zouaves were not to be daunted; and leaving the ground dotted with their dead and dying comrades, on they rushed, a wild cheer rising from their ranks, and a volley of balls pattering a reply. Again the line of fire burst from the dark stockade, and the advancing column withered away. The ground was strewn with fallen forms, and the fire of the stockade fell fast and sure. The men gave way, seeking the shelter of the bushes; their officers dashing to the front, vainly attempting to lead them on. It was useless, — even the sturdy Zouaves refused to cross the deadly slope, for to do so was death; on the green slope, across which the balls hurried fast and thick, lay whole ranks of French uniforms.

" The fire from stockade and bush raged fast and furious; well kept up on the side of the French, more deadly on that of the Kabyles, and still *the men would not advance* over the uncovered space, for it was certain death. Two thousand Kabyle marksmen lined the loop-holes, and the balls now began to whiz round the heads of the generals and their staff."

General MacMahon, who was wounded in this engagement, at last resorted to shells to dislodge the defenders; the result was successful, and the whole ended in a panic.

"Fast and furious now became the flight of the Kabyles, and all was havoc and confusion. The men of the Legion, mixed up with the Zouaves and the 54th, dashed after the fugitives, entering the villages with them, and bayoneting right and left with savage shouts, whilst down the steep sides of the hills, away over the ridges to the right and to the left, the waving bournous might be seen in flight!"

The curtain fell upon the Kabyle war soon after this action, and large detachments of troops were at once told off to build the fort. All around, on every promontory and hill, the little white tents were scattered thickly, and the sound of the bugle, and the sight of the red kepis of the soldiers, prevailed everywhere. But the war was practically over, civilians came up from Algiers, — some to see, and some to trade, — and quite a little colony sprung up. And here, on one of the heights shown in our next sketch, we establish ourselves again. Whilst Kabyle villages still smoulder in the distance, and revenge is deep in the hearts of insurgent tribes, "one peaceful English tent" is pitched upon the heights of Beni-Raten, and its occupants devote themselves to the uneventful pursuit of studying mountain beauty. We endeavor (and with some success) to ignore the military element; we listen neither to the réveille, nor to the too frequent crack of a rifle; our pursuits are not warlike, and, judging from the sights and sounds that sometimes surround us, we trust they never may be.

The view from this elevation is superb, —

north, south, east, and west, there is a wondrous
landscape, but northward especially; where, far
above the purple hills, higher than all but a few
snowy peaks, there stretches a horizontal line of
blue, that seems almost in the clouds. Nothing
gives us such a sense of height and distance as
these accidental peeps of the Mediterranean, and
nothing could contrast more effectively than the
snowy peaks in sunlight against the blue sea.

All this we are able to study in perfect security and with very little interruption; sketching

first one mountain-side clothed with a mass of verdure; another, rocky, barren, and wild; one day an olive-grove, another a deserted Kabyle village, and so on, with an infinite variety which would only be wearisome in detail. And we obtain what is so valuable to an artist, and what is supposed to be so rare in Africa, — variety of atmospheric effect. It is generally admitted (and we should be unwilling to contest the point) that English landscape is unrivalled in this respect, and that it is only *form* and *color* that we may study with advantage in tropical climates; but it should be remembered that, directly we ascend the mountains we lose the still, serene atmosphere that has been called the "monotony of blue."

We read often of African sun, but very seldom of African clouds and wind. To-day we are surrounded by clouds *below* us, which come and gather round the mountain-peaks and remain until

evening. Sometimes, just before sunset, the curtain will be lifted for a moment, and the hillsides will be in a blaze of gold, — again the
clouds come round, and do not disperse till
nightfall; and when the mountains are once
more revealed, the moon is up, and they are
of a silver hue, — the sky immediately above
remaining quite unclouded. The air is soft
on these half-clouded days, in spite of our
height above the sea; and the showers that
fall at intervals turn the soil in the valleys
into a hot-bed for forcing the gigantic vegetation.

The weather was nearly always fine, and we
generally found a little military tent (lent to us
by one of the Staff) sufficient protection and
shelter, even on this exposed situation. But we
must not forget the winds that lived in the
valleys, and came up to where our tents were
pitched, — sometimes one at a time, sometimes

three or four together. Of all things that impressed us during our stay upon the Kabyle hills, the beauty of the clouds, the purple tints upon the mountains, and the *wind*, will be remembered best. It is a common phrase, to speak of "scattering to the four winds"; but here the four winds came and met near our little camp, and sometimes made terrible havoc with our belongings. They came suddenly one day, and took up a tent, and flung it at a man and killed him; another time they came sighing gently, as if a light breeze were all we need prepare for, and in five minutes we found ourselves in the thick of a fight for our possessions, if not for our lives. And with the wind there came sometimes such sheets of rain, that turned the paths into watercourses, and carried shrubs and trees down into the valley; all this happening whilst the sea was calm in the distance, and the sun was shining fiercely on the plains. These were rough days, to be expected in late autumn and early spring, but not to be missed for a little personal discomfort, for Algeria has not been seen without a mountain storm.

Before leaving Kabylia, we will take one or two leaves from our note-book; just to picture to the reader, who may be more interested in what is going on at the Fort than in the various phases of the landscape, the rather incongruous elements of which our little society is made up.

Around the camp this evening there are groups of men and women standing, that bring forcibly to the mind those prints of the early patriarchs from which we are apt to take our first, and perhaps most vivid, impressions of Eastern life; and we cannot wonder at French artists attempting to illustrate Scriptural scenes from incidents in Algeria. There are Jacob and Joseph, as one might imagine them, to the life; Ruth in the

fields, and Rachel by the well; and there is a
patriarch coming down the mountain, with a light
about his head, as the sun's last rays burst upon
him, that Herbert might well have seen when
he was painting Moses with the tables of the law.
The effect is accidental, but it is perfect in an
artistic sense, from the solemnity of the man, the
attitude of the crowd of followers, the grand mountain forms which are partially lit up by gleams
of sunset, and the sharp shadows cast by the
throng.

This man may have been a warrior chief, or
the head of a tribe; he was certainly the head
of a large family, who pressed round him to an-
ticipate his wants and do him honor. His children seemed to be everywhere about him; they
were his furniture, they warmed his tent and kept
out the wind, they begged for him, prayed for
him, and generally helped him on his way. In
the Koran there is a saying of similar purport

to the words "happy is the man that hath his quiver full of them," — this one had his quiver full of them indeed, and whether he had ever done much to deserve the blessing, he certainly enjoyed it to the full.* Looked upon as a colored statue, he was, in some respects, a perfect type of beauty, strength, and dignified repose, — what we might fitly call a "study," as he sat waiting, whilst the women prepared his evening meal ; but whether from a moral point of view he quite deserved all the respect and deference that was paid to him, is another question.

As a picture, as we said before, he was magnificent, and there was a regal air with which he disposed the folds of his bournous, which we,

* How many a man is sheltered from the winds of the world by a grove of sleek relations, who surround him and keep him from harm ! Such a man has never really tried the outer world, and has but a second-hand experience of its troubles.

clad in the costume of advanced civilization, could
not but admire and envy. He had the advantage of us in every way, and made us feel it
acutely. He had a splendid arm, and we could
see it; the fine contour and color of his head
and neck were surrounded by white folds, but
not concealed. His head was not surmounted
with a battered "wide-awake," his neck was not
bandaged as if it were wounded, his feet were
not misshapen clumps of leather, his robes —
But we have no heart to go further into detail.
There is a "well-dressed" French gentleman standing near this figure; and there is not about him
one graceful fold, one good suggestive line, one
tint of color grateful to the eye, or one re-
deeming feature in his (by contrast) hideous *tout
ensemble.*

These are every-day truths, but they strike us
sometimes with a sort of surprise; we have discovered no new thing in costume, and nothing

worth telling; but the sudden and humiliating contrast gives our artistic sensibilities a shock, and fills us with despair.

A little way removed there is a warrior on horseback at prayers, his hands outstretched, his face turned towards the sun. It is as grand a picture as the last, but it does not bear examination. He came and sat down afterwards, to smoke, close to our tent, and we regret to say that he was extremely dirty, and in his habits rather cruel. There were red drops upon the ground where his horse had stood, and his spur was a terrible instrument to contemplate; in the enthusiasm of a noble nature he had ridden his delicate locomotive too hard, and had sometimes forgotten to give it a feed. It was a beautiful, black Arab steed, but it wanted grooming sadly; its feet were cracked and spread from neglect, and its whole appearance betokened rough usage. Perhaps this was an exceptional case, perhaps not; but to the scandal of those whose romantic picture of the Arab in his tent with his children and his steed are amongst the most cherished associations, we are bound to confess that we have seen as much cruelty as kindness bestowed by the Arabs and Kabyles on their horses, and incline to the opinion that they are, as a rule, anything but tender and loving to their four-footed friends.

The Kabyles came round our tents in the morning before leaving, and the last we saw of our model patriarch he was flying before an en-raged vivandière, who pursued him down the hill with a dishcloth. He had been prowling about since dawn, and had forgotten the distinc-tion between "meum" and "tuum."

It has been said that there is "no such thing as Arab embarrassment, and no such dignity as Arab dignity"; but the Arab or the Kabyle, as we hinted in a former chapter, appears to great disadvantage in contact with the French, and seems to lose at once in *morale.*

Another day, there is a flutter in our little camp, for "the mail" has come in, in the person of an active young orderly of Zouaves, who, leaving the bulk of his charge to come round by the road, has anticipated the regular delivery by some hours, scaling the heights with the agility of a cat, and appearing suddenly in our midst. If he had sprung out of the earth he could not have startled us much more, and if he had brought a message that all the troops were to leave Africa to-morrow, he could scarcely have been more welcome.

And what has he brought to satisfy the crowd of anxious faces that assemble round the hut, dignified by the decoration of a pasteboard eagle and the inscription " *Bureau de Poste* " ? It was scarcely as trying a position for an official as

9   M

that at our own Post-office at Sebastopol in Cri-
mean days, although there was eagerness and
crowding enough to perplex any distributor; but
it was very soon over, in five minutes letters and
papers were cast aside, and boredom had recom-
menced with the majority. It was the old
story, — the old curse of Algeria doing its work;
the French officers are too near home to care
much for "news," and hear too frequently from
Paris (twice a week) to attach much importance
to letters. Newspapers were the "pièces de ré-
sistance," but there was not much news in "*La
Presse,*" and its *feuilleton* consisted of two or
three chapters of a translation of Dickens's "Mar-
tin Chuzzlewit"; there was the "*Moniteur,*" with
lists of promotions in the army, and the usual
announcement that "NAPOLEON, by the grace
of God and the national will," would levy new
taxes upon the people; there was a provincial
paper, containing an account of the discovery of

some ruins near Carcassonne; there was "*Le Follet*" for "my lady *commandant*," and a few other papers with illustrated caricatures and conundrums.

Some of the letters were amusing, as we heard them read aloud; one was too quaint not to mention: it was from a boot-maker in Paris to his dear, long-lost customer on the Kabyle hills. He "felt that he was going to die," and prayed "*M'sieu le Lieutenant*" to order a good supply of boots for fear of any sudden accident; "no one else could make such boots for Monsieur." And so on, including subjects of about equal importance, with the latest Parisian gossip, and intelligence of a new piece at the "Variétés." One other letter we may mention, that came up by the same post to a member of that little band perched like eagles on the heights; it was also unimportant, but from *home*, in England; the burden of it was this, — "BROADTOUCH" had stretched ten feet of canvas for a painting of one rolling wave, and "INTERSTICE" had studied the texture of a nutshell until his eyes were dim!

We finish the evening as usual with dominoes and coffee; enjoying many a long and delightful chit-chat with our military friends. These pleasant, genial, but rather unhappy gentlemen do not "talk shop"; it is tabooed in conversation, as strictly as at the "Rag": but the stamp of banishment is upon their faces unmistakably, and if they do speak of the service in answer to a question, it is in language that seems to say, "All ye who enter here leave Hope behind." But opinions happily differ very widely; *we* were reluctant to leave the Fort.

The Imperial Eagle crowned the heights of Beni-Raten, the red kepis was dotted thickly amongst the green foliage, the bugle was heard from several hills, as we went down the military

road for the last time. It was late in the evening before we arrived at Tiziouzou, and the last
figure that we saw in Kabylia — the last man
that dwells in our recollection — was neither Arab
nor Kabyle. In the half light it might have been
some antediluvian bird that haunted this region ;
at any rate it added to our experience of the " confusion of styles " with which this country abounds.

WINTER SWALLOWS.

CHAPTER IX.

"WINTER SWALLOWS."

"Oh que l'hirondelle est bien la type de la vraie sagesse, elle qui a su effacer de son existence, ces longs hivers qui glacent et engourdissent! Dès que le soleil commence à décroître, sitôt que les plantes jaunissent et qu'aux chaudes haleines du Zéphyr succèdent les froides rafales de l'aquilon, elle s'envole prudemment à tire d'ailes, vers les douces régions embaumées du Midi."

WE come down the hills and back to Algiers, to find the winter in full bloom, and the "winter swallows" in great force. In fact, so full of bustle is the town, and so frequent is the sight of English faces, and so familiar the sound of voices, that it hardly seems like the place we had left a few weeks since.

It has been said that English people love sunshine and blue sky more than any other nation, and that the dwellers under the " ciel nebuleuse du nord" will go anywhere to seek a brighter clime; and it is a fact, the importance of which is hardly realized, that the African sun is producing a crop of residents that is taking firm root in the soil in spite of siroccos, in spite of earthquakes, without a thought of colonization in the strict sense of the word, and without, it must be added, any particular love for the French people.

As the visitors and tourists are increasing, they are naturally rather vulgarizing our favorite places. Thus we hear of picnics at the Bouzareah, of balls at Mustapha, of "trips" to Blidah by railway, and of "excursions to the gorge of La Chiffa and back" in one day. An amusing chapter might be written upon Algiers from the traveller's point of view, but one or two touches will suffice to show the easy and familiar terms on which our countrymen and countrywomen invade this stronghold of the French; once the "city of pirates" and the terror of Mediterranean waters.

There is the American traveller, who, having "done Europe," finds Algiers, of course, rather "slow" by contrast; and there is the very matter-of-fact traveller, who finds it all vanity, and says, "Take ever so copious a stock of illusions with you to the bright Orient, and within half an hour after landing you are as bankrupt as a bank of deposit; .... and the end of it all is, that this city of the 'Arabian Nights' turns out to be as unromantic as Seven Dials." There are lady travellers, who (enjoying special advantages by reason of their sex, and seeing much more than Englishmen of Moorish interiors) are perhaps best fitted to write books about this country; there are proselytizing ladies, who come with a mission, and end by getting themselves and their friends into trouble by distributing tracts amongst the Moors; and there are ladies who (when their baggage is

9 *

detained at one of the ports) endeavor to break down the barriers of official routine in an unexpected way. "The douâne did not choose to wake up and give us our luggage," writes one, "it was such a lazy douâne; and though I went again and again and said pretty things to the gendarmes, it was of no use."

Another form of invasion is less polite, but it has been submitted to with tolerable grace on more than one occasion. Here is the latest instance, taken from "Under the Palms," by the Hon. Lewis Wingfield.

"Being anxious," he says, "to obtain a sketch of one of the quaint streets of the upper town, I wandered one morning up its dark alleys and intricate by-ways; and wishing to establish myself at a window, I knocked at a promising door, and was answered by a mysterious voice from behind a lattice; the door opened of itself, and I marched up stairs unmindful of evil. In the

upper court I was instantly surrounded by a troup
of women in the picturesque private dress of the
Moorish ladies, unencumbered with veil or yashmak.

" These ladies dragged at my watch-chain and
pulled my hair, until, finding myself in such
very questionable society, I beat a hasty retreat,
flying down stairs six steps at a time, slamming
the doors in the faces of the houris, and event-
ually reaching the street in safety, while sundry
slow Mussulmans wagged their beards and said
that Christian dogs did not often enter such
places with impunity."

It is pleasant to see with what good-tempered
grace both the Moors and the French take this
modern invasion. We settle down for the winter here and build and plant vineyards, and
make merry in the same romping fashion that
we do in Switzerland. We write to England
about it as if the country belonged to us, and
of the climate as if we had been the discoverers

of its charms. But it is all so cosey and genial, and so much a matter of course, that we are apt to forget its oddity; we have friends who speak of Algiers with positive delight, whose faces brighten at the very mention of its name, and who always speak of going there as of "going home."

We have principally confined our remarks to places near Algiers, omitting all mention of Oran and Constantine, because it is impossible to work to much purpose if we travel about, and these places are worthy of distinct and separate visits. The longest journey that we would suggest to artists to make in one winter would be to the cedar forests of Teniet-el-Hâd, because the scenery is so magnificent, and the forms of the cedars themselves are perhaps the wildest and most wonderful to be met with in any part of the world. Hitherto, almost the only sketches that we have seen of this mountain forest have been by our own countrymen and countrywomen, for French artists do not as a rule go far from Algiers.

With a few notable exceptions,* our experience of the works of Frenchmen in Algiers has
been anything but inspiring; we have known
these artists closeted for weeks, — copying and
recopying fanciful desert scenes, such as camels
dying on sandy plains, under a sky of the heavi-
est opaque blue, and with cold gray shadows
upon the ground, — drawing imaginary Mauresques on impossible house-tops, and, in short,
working more from fancy than from facts; producing, it may be, most salable pictures, but
doing themselves and their *clientelles* no other
good thereby. It seems ungracious to speak
thus of people from whom we invariably received civility and kindness; but the truth re-
mains, we found them hard at work on "pot-
boilers" for exportation, and doing, like the
photographers, a flourishing trade.

* We shall not be accused of alluding in this category to
such painters as the late Horace Vernêt, or to Gérome and
others who study here in winter time.

We should endeavor to spend most of our time in the country, if we wish to make progress. If we stay in Algiers we shall of course be liable to some interruptions; we shall be too comfortable and perhaps become too luxurious. We must not dream away our time on a Turkey carpet, or on our *terrasse*, charming though the view may be. There is too much scent of henna, too strong a flavor of coffee and tobacco, there are, in short, too many of the comforts of life; we had better be off to the hills, where the air is cooler, and where we can live a free life under canvas for a while.*

A few months spent amongst the mountains

* It may not be thought very practical to suggest much sketching in the open air, as the light is generally considered too trying, and the glare too great, for any very successful work in color. But the tropical vegetation in Algeria gives continual shade and shelter, and the style of architecture, with cool open arcades to the houses, is admirably adapted for work ; and, failing the ordinary means of shelter, much may be done under a large umbrella or an ordinary military tent.

has a wonderfully bracing effect on Europeans, because both the eye and the mind are satisfied and refreshed; although it is a curious fact to note that on the uneducated such scenes have little or no influence. We shall not easily forget "the splendid comet of Arab civilization that has left such a trail of light behind it," but cannot help remarking that neither the Arab in a state of nature, nor the Moor surrounded by every refinement and luxury, seems to be much influenced by the grace and beauty around them; and in this they do not stand alone, for it is, as we said, a notable fact, that contact with what is beautiful in scenery or in art is of itself of little worth.

What shall we say of the Sicilian peasant-girl, born and bred on the heights of Taormina, — what of the Swiss girl who spends her days knee-deep in newly mown hay? Does beautiful scenery seem to inspire them with noble thoughts, — does being "face to face with Nature" (as the phrase goes) appear to give them refined tastes, or to elevate their ideas? Does it seem to lead to cleanliness, to godliness, or any other virtue? The answer is almost invariably, "No"; they must be educated to it, and neither the present race of Arabs or Moors are so educated. They do not seem to appreciate the works of their fathers, and will, probably before long, fall into the way of dressing themselves and building dwellings after the style of their conquerors.

With Europeans it is just the reverse, and the most educated and refined amongst us are learning more and more to value what Eastern nations are casting off. We submit to the fashions of our time not without murmurs, which are sounds of hope; we put up with a hideous costume and more hideous streets, — from habit or necessity, as the case may be, — but even custom will not altogether deaden the senses to a

love for the beautiful. In costume this is especially noticeable. What is it that attracts the
largest audiences to "burlesque" representations
at our theatres? Not the buffoonery, but the
spectacle. The eye, robbed of its natural food,
seeks it in a number of roundabout ways, — but
it seeks it. What made the American people
crowd to Ristori's performances in New York
over and over again? Not the novelty, not alone
for the sake of being able to say that they had
been there, but for the delight to the eye in
contemplating forms of classic beauty, and the
delight to the ear in hearing the poetry of the
most musical language in the world nobly spoken,
although but few of the audience could understand a word. It was a libel upon the people to
suggest that their attending these performances
was affectation; it was an almost unconscious
drawing out of that love for the beautiful which
is implanted somewhere in every human breast.

N

CONCLUSION.

CHAPTER X.

CONCLUSION.

IF the foregoing sketches have seemed to some of our readers a thought too slight and discursive, and to be wanting in detail, it is because, perhaps, they have reflected a little too naturally the habit of a painter's mind, and have followed out the principle of outdoor sketching, which is to "hit off" as accurately as possible the various points of interest that come under observation, and, in doing so, to give *color* rather than detail, and to aim principally at the rendering of atmosphere and effect.

But for this, perhaps, most readers will be thankful, and for two reasons. First, because it

is a fact that English and American people care
little or nothing for Algeria as a colony, — that
they never have cared, and probably never will.
Second, because, in spite of the assertion of a late
writer that " Algeria is a country virtually unknown," we believe that the reading public has
been inundated with books of travel and statistics
on this subject.

It is only in its picturesque aspect, and as a
winter residence for invalids, that Algiers will
ever claim much interest for English people ; and
even in picturesqueness it falls far short of other
cities of the East.   There is nothing in costume
to compare with the bazaars of Constantinople, or
in architecture to the by-streets of Trebizond ; but
Algeria is much more accessible, and that is our
reason for selecting it.   And it has one special at-
traction, in which it stands almost alone, namely,
that here we may see the two great tides of civilization — the primitive and modern, the East and

the West — meet and mingle without limit and without confusion. There is no violent collision and no decided fusion ; but the general result is peaceful, and we are enabled to contemplate it at leisure, and have such intimate and quiet intercourse with the Oriental as is nowhere else to be met with, we believe, in the world.

In fine, for artists Algiers seems perfect ; a cheap place of residence with few "distractions," without many taxes or cares ; with extraordinary opportunities for the study of Nature in her grandest aspects, and of character, costume, and architecture of a good old type.

But what they really gain by working here is not easily written down, nor to be explained to others ; nor is it all at once discovered by themselves. It has not been dinned into their ears by rote, or by rule, but rather inhaled, and (if we may so express it) taken in with the atmosphere they breathe. If they have not produced

anything great or noble, they have at least in-
fused more light and nature into their work, and
have done something to counteract the tendency
to that sickly sentimentality and artificialism
that is the curse of modern schools.

We have been led to insist, perhaps a little
too earnestly, on the good effects of sound work
on a painter's mind, by the thought of what some
of our foremost artists are doing at the present
time. When painters of the highest aim and
most refined intelligence seem tending towards
a system of mere decorative art; when Millais
paints children, apparently, to display their dress,
and devotes his great powers as a colorist to
dexterous imitation; when Leighton cultivates a
style of refined Platonism which is not Attic and
is sometimes scarcely human; when other painters
of celebrity, that we need scarcely name, spend
their lives upon the working out of effective de-

tails; when the modern development of what is called Pre-Raphaelitism seems to remove us farther than ever from what should be the aim of a great painter, — we may be pardoned for insisting upon the benefits of change of air and change of scene.

But not only to artists and amateurs, — to those fortunate people whose time and means are as much at their own disposal as the genii of Aladdin's lamp; to those who can get "ordered abroad" at the season when it is most pleasant to go; to those who live at high pressure for half the year, and need a change, not so much perhaps from winter's gloom as from the clouds that linger on the mind's horizon; to all who seek a new sensation, we would say once more, — pay a visit to the "city of pirates," to the diamond set in emeralds, on the African shore.

Cambridge: Electrotyped and Printed by Welch, Bigelow, & Co.

OVER 100,000 COPIES OF THIS WORK HAVE BEEN SOLD IN FRENCH.

Guizot's Popular History of France.

TRANSLATED BY ROBERT BLACK.

This great Work is now offered to the American public, and the Publishers, having spared no pains or expense in its reproduction, confidently believe that, as a specimen of book-making, it is unexcelled by ANY BOOK MADE IN AMERICA. By a special arrangement with the European publishers, we have secured Electrotypes of ALL OF THE ORIGINAL WOOD CUTS, by the celebrated artist, A. DE NEUVILLE, thereby securing impressions of the same fully equal to the originals. These Three Hundred Illustrations are pronounced by some of the best Art judges in the country to be the FINEST WOOD CUTS EVER PRINTED IN AMERICA. Besides the above, we have added to the work FORTY MAGNIFICENT STEEL LINE ENGRAVINGS, by celebrated artists.

Persons wanting a GOOD and RELIABLE History of France, need have no hesitation in subscribing for this, as it is the ONLY ONE of a popular nature, and by a STANDARD HISTORIAN, to be had in the English language. The Publishers offer it confidently believing that it will supply a long-felt want. The world-wide reputation of GUIZOT is a sufficient recommendation to the work, and a guarantee of its being a thoroughly correct and an intensely interesting history.

☞ Experienced canvassers wanted for this magnificent work. Apply to the publishers.

Fifty-five parts, paper, ...	$27.50
Six large royal octavo vols. :—	
·Cloth, extra, ...	33.00
Full sheep (library) marbled edges, . .	39.00
Half calf, gilt, extra, ...	. 45.00
Half morocco, extra, ...	45.00
Full morocco, gilt, extra, . . .	60.00
Full tree calf, gilt extra, . . .	60.00

TESTIMONIALS.

———◦◦———

Boston, Nov. 20, 1873.

Gentlemen: M. Guizot's History of France should be read by all who are not indifferent to historical studies. To a most interesting subject he brings the experience of a statesman, the study of a professor, and the charm of an accomplished writer. I am glad you are to place this recent work within the reach of all American readers.

Faithfully yours,   CHARLES SUMNER.

———

Everything from the pen of Guizot is remarkable for thoroughness of investigation and exact statement.   WENDELL PHILLIPS.

———

The work supplies a want which has long been felt, and it ought to be in the hands of all students of history. We cannot doubt that it will meet with the same favorable reception in England which has already attended its publication in France.   LONDON TIMES.

———

The name of Guizot is a sufficient guarantee for the historical value of whatever he writes.   E. G. ROBINSON, Pres. Brown University.

———

I should be glad to see Guizot's History of France in every school.
JOHN D. PHILBRICK, Sup't Public Schools, Boston.

———

The Popular History of France will be interesting, instructive, and worth to intelligent persons much more than it will cost.
W. A. STEARNS, Pres. Amherst College.

———

I have no hesitation in recommending this work.
JOHN W. BURGESS, Prof. History Amherst College.

———

There is no man more fit to write a History of France than M. Guizot.
JOSHUA L. CHAMBERLIN, President Bowdoin College.

———

We have seen no other subscription book which, for literary, artistic, and mechanical excellence, could be so unreservedly commended.
MICHIGAN TEACHER.

Packard's Guide to the Study of Insects.

Being a popular Introduction to the Study of Entomology, and a Treatise on Injurious and Beneficial Insects; with Descriptions and Accounts of the Habits of Insects, their Transformations, Development, and Classification. 15 full-page Plates, and 670 Cuts in the Text, embracing 1260 Figures of American Insects. Fifth edition. 1 vol. 8vo. Price reduced to $5.00.

This book is now acknowledged to be *the standard*, and is used in the leading universities and institutions of Europe and America.

Half Hours with Insects.

A Popular Account of their Habits, Modes of Life, &c., &c. By A. S. PACKARD, JR. of the Peabody Academy of Science. The subjects treated are — Insects of the Garden, of the Plant-House, of our Ponds and Brooks; Population of an Apple Tree; Insects of the Forest, as Musicians and Mimics, as Architects; Insects in Societies; the Reasoning Powers of Insects. Twelve parts, fully illustrated; each part 25 cts. One vol. Crown 8vo. Cloth. $2.50.

Say's Entomology.

A Description of the Insects of North America. By THOMAS SAY. With 54 full-page steel-plate Illustrations, engraved and colored from nature. Edited by J. L. LE CONTE. With a Memoir by GEO. ORD. Two vols. 8vo. Cloth, $15.00; half calf, $20 00.

This standard work is now out of print, the plates having been destroyed. We offer the balance of the edition at the above prices. It will soon become scarce, and command a very much higher price.

Our Common Insects.

A popular Account of the more common Insects of our Country, embracing chapters on Bees and their Parasites, Moths, Flies, Mosquitos, Beetles, &c.; while a Calendar will give a general Account of the more common Injurious and Beneficial Insects, and their Time of Appearance, Habits, &c. 224 pp. New edition. Profusely illustrated. 1 vol. Cloth. $1.50.